Travel Guide to Tbilisi, G

Welcome to the captivating heart of Georgia - **Tbilisi**. A city where diverse cultures, rich history, and warm-hearted people blend into a memorable travel experience, Tbilisi is an undiscovered gem awaiting the discerning traveler. This comprehensive guide aims to equip you with all the tools necessary to unravel the intricate tapestry of experiences Tbilisi offers, from the tranquillity of its ancient monasteries to the dynamic energy of its burgeoning nightlife.

In this guide, you will find an in-depth exploration of Tbilisi's **geography**, **population**, **language**, and **culture**. We take you through the city's key attractions, unveiling interesting facts about the capital that could surprise even the seasoned traveler. Expect to delve into the *tantalizing food culture*, celebrated for its unique flavors and traditional recipes that have stood the test of time. Our **detailed maps** will aid you in navigating the city effortlessly, giving you the liberty to create your own adventure within the old city walls or in the modern quarters of Tbilisi. Wondering when to visit? We've got you covered. Our guide helps you identify the **best time to visit** Tbilisi based on your personal preferences.

For those planning longer stays, we provide tailor-made itineraries, including **day trips** and **excursions** that promise to showcase the best of Tbilisi and its environs. If you're constrained by time, our section on 'One Day in Tbilisi' provides a condensed itinerary ensuring you don't miss out on the must-see spots.

From getting around, understanding **visa requirements**, selecting where to stay, to pinpointing which markets to explore for unique souvenirs - all these essentials and much more are included in this guide. Not to mention a deep dive into Tbilisi's **art scene**, **theatre culture**, and **museums**, for those yearning for a cultural feast. Lastly, the guide offers **practical tips**, including safety precautions and respect for local customs, to ensure your visit to Tbilisi is enjoyable, safe, and respectful to the local community.

In essence, this guide is your all-access pass to the treasures of Tbilisi, and we hope it inspires you to explore this captivating city with an open heart and curious mind. *Get ready to fall in love with Tbilisi, one page at a time.*

Table of Contents

- 1.1 Introduction 6
- 1.2 Map of Georgia 9
- 1.3 Map of Eastern Europe 10
- 1.4 Map of Tbilisi 10
- 1.5 A History of Tbilisi 11
- 1.6 The Population of Tbilisi 12
- 1.7 Languages of Tbilisi and common phrases 14
- 1.8 The Culture and Religions of Tbilisi 15
- 1.9 Currency in Tbilisi 16
- 1.10 Geography and Climate of Tbilisi 18
- 1.11 Best time to visit Tbilisi 19
- 1.12 Key attractions in Tbilisi 20
- 1.13 Interesting facts about Tbilisi 21
- 1.14 FAQ's when travelling to Tbilisi 23
- 1.15 Safety precautions 24
- 2 Getting to Tbilisi 26
  - 2.1 Visa requirements and Entry Regulations 26
  - 2.2 Traveling to Tbilisi 26
  - 2.3 Transport from the airports 28
  - 2.4 Public Transportation in Tbilisi 28
  - 2.5 Car Rentals and Driving 30
  - 2.6 Tour Companies 31
  - 2.7 Other means of getting around 32
- 3 Where to stay in Tbilisi 34
  - 3.1 Districts in Tbilisi 34
  - 3.2 Hotels in Tbilisi 36
- 4 Food Culture of Tbilisi 42
  - 4.1 Traditional Food from Tbilisi 42

- 4.2 Food served during Religious Holidays 48
- 4.3 Restaurants in Tbilisi 49
- 4.4 Markets 50
- 5 Shopping in Tbilisi 51
- 6 Top Attractions in Tbilisi 54
  - 6.1 Narikala Fortress 54
  - 6.2 Tbilisi Old Town: A Journey Through History 55
  - 6.3 The Bridge of Peace 56
  - 6.4 The Holy Trinity Cathedral of Tbilisi 58
  - 6.5 Mtatsminda Park 60
  - 6.6 The Georgian National Museum 61
  - 6.7 The Tbilisi Sea 62
  - 6.8 The National Botanical Garden of Georgia 64
  - 6.9 Abanotubani: A Historic Gem in the Heart of Tbilisi .. 65
- 7 Culture and Entertainment in Tbilisi 67
  - 7.1 Art Galleries 67
  - 7.2 Museums 68
  - 7.3 Theatres 69
  - 7.4 Nightlife in Tbilisi 70
- 8 Day Trips and Excursions 72
  - 8.1 One Day in Tbilisi Itinerary 72
  - 8.2 Tbilisi: Kazbegi Full-Day Group Tour 73
  - 8.3 From Tbilisi: Day Trip to Armenia 76
  - 8.4 Jvari Monastery, Ananuri, Gudauri, and Kazbegi Tour 77
- 9 3 Days in Tbilisi 80
  - 9.1 Day One 80
  - 9.2 Day Two 82
  - 9.3 Day Three 83
- 10 Practical Tips for Visiting Tbilisi 84

10.1	Currency	84
10.2	Language	84
10.3	Safety	84
10.4	Dress Code	84
10.5	Transportation	85
10.6	Food and Water	85
10.7	Connectivity	85
10.8	Weather	85
10.9	Sightseeing	85
10.10	Respect Local Customs	85
11	Conclusion	86

1.1 Introduction

Welcome to Tbilisi, the vibrant, beating heart of Georgia, where the past and present coalesce in a dance of culture, cuisine, and captivating charm. This city, nestled in the valley of the Mtkvari River and framed by the picturesque Caucasus Mountains, is a hidden gem waiting to be discovered.

Tbilisi, Georgia's capital, is a city of contrasts. Its rich history dates back to the 5th century, and it has been a melting pot of influences from Europe, Asia, and the Middle East. This eclectic mix is evident in the city's architecture, where medieval, classical, and Soviet structures stand side by side, creating a unique cityscape that tells a thousand tales.

As you wander through the narrow, winding streets of the Old Town, you'll be transported back in time. Here, you'll find the ancient Narikala Fortress, standing guard over the city, and the iconic Metekhi Church, perched on a cliff overlooking the river. The charming, traditional houses with their wooden balconies, the sulphur baths that have been a part of Tbilisi's culture for centuries, and the cobblestone streets all contribute to the Old Town's enchanting atmosphere.

But Tbilisi is not just about the past. The city is also a burgeoning modern metropolis. The futuristic Bridge of Peace, made of glass and steel, is a testament to Tbilisi's forward-thinking spirit. The city's skyline is dotted with modern architecture, and its streets are lined with trendy cafes, boutiques, and art galleries. Tbilisi's cultural scene is thriving, with a plethora of museums, theaters, and music venues offering a diverse array of entertainment.

Tbilisi is also a gastronomic paradise. Georgian cuisine is a delightful fusion of flavors from East and West. From the hearty khinkali (dumplings) and the cheesy goodness of khachapuri to the unique flavors of Georgian wine, your taste buds are in for a treat. The city's burgeoning food scene offers everything from traditional Georgian eateries to modern, fusion restaurants.

Nature lovers will not be disappointed either. The city's location at the foot of the Trialeti mountain range offers plenty of opportunities for hiking and exploration. The verdant Mtatsminda Park, the tranquil Turtle Lake, and the botanical garden are perfect for those seeking a respite from the city's hustle and bustle.

Tbilisi is a city of warmth, not just in its sulphur baths, but in its people. Georgians are known for their hospitality, and Tbilisians are no exception. The city's vibrant, welcoming spirit is infectious, and you'll find yourself feeling at home in no time.

Tbilisi is more than just a destination; it's an experience. It's a city where every corner holds a new discovery, where the old and new coexist harmoniously, and where every moment is steeped in rich, cultural flavor. Whether you're a history buff, a foodie, a culture vulture, or a nature lover, Tbilisi has something to offer you.

So come, immerse yourself in the magic of Tbilisi, and let this charming city weave its spell around you. Discover its secrets, savor its flavors, and let its rhythm move you. Tbilisi is not just a city to be seen; it's a city to be felt, to be lived, and to be loved. Welcome to Tbilisi, where every visit is a journey, and every journey is a story waiting to be told.

1.2 Map of Georgia

Situated at the crossroads of Europe and Asia, the majestic nation of Georgia resides within the Southern Caucasus. To its west, you'll find the shimmering Black Sea that separates it from Bulgaria and Romania. North of the country, the formidable landscapes of Russia stretch far and wide, embodying a shared history marked by complex relations, both amicable and contentious. This history of cultural exchange, conflict, and compromise echoes across the region.

To the south, Georgia is bordered by Turkey, Armenia, and Azerbaijan, each adding a vibrant thread to the intricate tapestry of Georgia's geopolitical and cultural milieu. Turkey, with its powerful influence and shared Black Sea coastline, represents a crucial economic partner and a source of tourists. Simultaneously, Georgia has been a theater for historic rivalries between Armenia and Azerbaijan, two countries with whom Georgia shares close cultural ties, but whose conflicts occasionally cast a shadow over the region.

Despite such challenges, these unique relationships have forged Georgia into a fascinating intersection of cultures, evident in Tbilisi's stunning architecture, food, and overall atmosphere. Here, Byzantine, Ottoman, Persian, and Soviet influences all converge, making it a genuinely diverse and captivating destination.

1.3 Map of Eastern Europe

The map below gives an indication of where Georgia is situated in Eastern Europe.

1.4 Map of Tbilisi

Interactive link to the map. Visit https://bit.ly/3DDB9vn

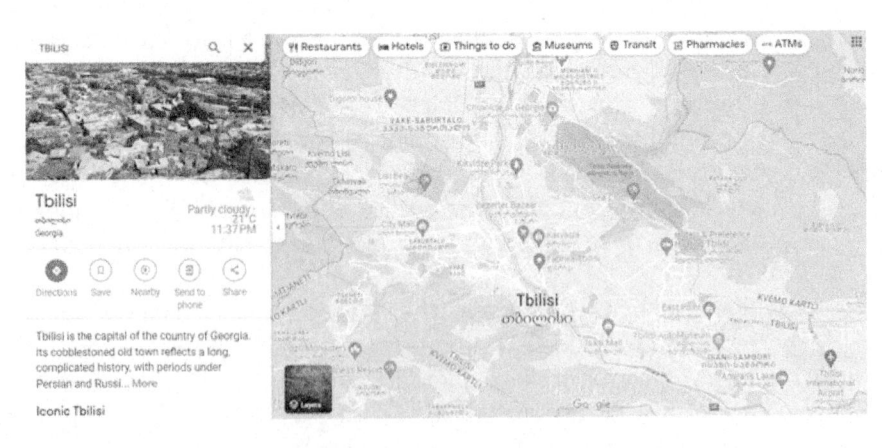

1.5 A History of Tbilisi

Tbilisi, the capital of Georgia, is a city steeped in history. Its story is a rich tapestry of conquests, cultural fusion, resilience, and rebirth. The city's history is a testament to its strategic importance and its enduring spirit.

Tbilisi's story begins in the 5th century AD when it was founded by King Vakhtang Gorgasali of Iberia. Legend has it that while hunting, the king's falcon caught a pheasant, and both birds fell into a hot spring and died. Struck by the discovery of the hot springs, the king decided to build a city on the site, and thus Tbilisi, which means 'warm location', was born.

Over the centuries, Tbilisi's strategic location made it a coveted prize for various empires. The Persians, Arabs, Byzantines, Mongols, and Ottomans all left their mark on the city. Each conquest brought with it a new layer of cultural influence, shaping Tbilisi's unique character.

The Arab conquest in the 7th century was particularly significant. The Arabs ruled Tbilisi for about four centuries, and it was during this period that the city became a significant cultural, political, and economic center. The influence of Arab culture is still evident in Tbilisi's architecture and traditions.

In the 12th and 13th centuries, under the rule of Queen Tamar, Georgia experienced a golden age. Tbilisi flourished as a hub of culture and commerce. However, this period of prosperity was short-lived. The Mongol invasion in the 13th century marked the beginning of a period of decline and turmoil for Tbilisi.

The city was repeatedly sacked and burned during the Timurid invasions in the 14th and 15th centuries. The subsequent centuries saw Tbilisi change hands multiple times between the Persians and Ottomans.

In 1801, Tbilisi and the rest of eastern Georgia were annexed by the Russian Empire. This period saw significant changes in the city's architecture, with European-style buildings replacing the traditional Persian and Ottoman structures. Tbilisi became the administrative and cultural center of the Caucasus.

The 20th century brought with it new challenges. Georgia declared independence in 1918, but this was short-lived. In 1921, the Red Army invaded Georgia, and Tbilisi became the capital of the Georgian Soviet Socialist Republic.

The collapse of the Soviet Union in 1991 marked a new chapter in Tbilisi's history. Georgia regained its independence, and Tbilisi once again became the capital of an independent Georgia. However, the transition was not smooth. The early years of independence were marked by economic instability and civil unrest.

Today, Tbilisi is a city in transformation. It's a city that's striving to balance its rich history with its aspirations for the future. Despite the challenges, Tbilisi has emerged as a vibrant, dynamic city. It's a city that's embracing modernity while staying true to its roots.

Tbilisi's history is a testament to its resilience. The city has endured countless invasions, conquests, and upheavals, yet it has always found a way to rise from the ashes. It's a city that's been shaped by its past, but it's not defined by it. Tbilisi's story is still being written, and its future is as promising as its past is rich.

As for the current situation, Tbilisi is a city on the move. It's a city that's rapidly modernizing and developing. The city's economy is growing, and it's becoming an increasingly popular tourist destination. Tbilisi is a city that's looking forward, but it's a city that will always remember its past. It's a city that's proud of its history, its culture, and its identity. And it's a city that's ready to welcome the world with open arms.

1.6 The Population of Tbilisi

Tbilisi, the capital city of Georgia, is a vibrant metropolis that is as diverse as it is dynamic. The city's population is a melting pot of different ethnicities, cultures, and religions, reflecting its rich history and strategic location at the crossroads of Europe and Asia.

As of the latest census, Tbilisi has a population of **approximately 1.5 million people**, making it the largest city in Georgia. The city is the country's political, economic, and cultural hub, and it's home to about a third of Georgia's total population.

Tbilisi's population is predominantly Georgian, but the city is also home to a diverse array of ethnic minorities. Armenians, Russians, Azerbaijanis, and other ethnic groups all contribute to the city's multicultural fabric. This diversity is a testament to Tbilisi's history as a city that has been influenced by various cultures and empires over the centuries.

The Georgian population in Tbilisi is diverse in itself, with people from different regions of Georgia bringing their unique customs, dialects, and traditions to the city. This regional diversity adds another layer to Tbilisi's multicultural character.

Religious diversity is another defining feature of Tbilisi's population. The majority of Tbilisians are Eastern Orthodox Christians, but the city is also home to significant Muslim, Armenian Apostolic, and Roman Catholic communities. There are also smaller communities of Jews, Yezidis, and other religious groups. This religious diversity is reflected in the city's architecture, with Orthodox churches, mosques, synagogues, and other places of worship standing side by side.

Tbilisi's population is also diverse in terms of age and socio-economic status. The city is home to a mix of young professionals, students, families, and retirees. It's a city where the old and the new coexist, with traditional markets and modern shopping malls, historic neighborhoods and new developments, street vendors and high-end boutiques.

In terms of the main towns in Tbilisi, the city is divided into several districts, each with its own unique character and population. Some of the main districts include:

Old Tbilisi: This is the historic heart of the city, known for its medieval architecture, cobblestone streets, and traditional sulfur baths. It's a popular tourist destination and a vibrant area with a mix of locals and tourists.

Vake-Saburtalo: This is a modern, upscale district known for its shopping centers, restaurants, and parks. It's also home to many of the city's universities and educational institutions.

Gldani-Nadzaladevi: This is one of the most populous districts in Tbilisi, known for its residential neighborhoods and local markets.

Didube-Chugureti: This district is a mix of residential and commercial areas, with a diverse population and a bustling street market.

Isani-Samgori: This district is home to a large Armenian community and is known for its historic churches and monasteries.

Tbilisi's population is as diverse as the city itself. It's a city that's shaped by its people, their cultures, their religions, and their stories. It's a city that's proud of its diversity and that celebrates it in every aspect of city life. Tbilisi is a city where everyone is welcome, and where everyone can find a place to call home.

1.7 Languages of Tbilisi and common phrases

Tbilisi, as the capital of Georgia, is a linguistic melting pot. The city's rich history and cultural diversity are reflected in the variety of languages spoken by its residents.

The official and most widely spoken language in Tbilisi is Georgian. Georgian is the native language of the Georgians, the largest ethnic group in the city. It's a unique language with its own alphabet, known as the Mkhedruli script, which is renowned for its elegance and beauty.

Despite Georgian being the dominant language, Tbilisi's multicultural character means that several other languages are also spoken in the city. These include Russian, Armenian, and Azerbaijani, reflecting the city's significant Russian, Armenian, and Azerbaijani communities. English is also increasingly spoken, particularly among the younger generation and in the tourism and hospitality sectors.

Here are some common Georgian phrases that might be useful for first-time visitors to Tbilisi.
- "Gamarjoba" - Hello
- "Madloba" - Thank you
- "Tu sheidzleba" - Please
- "Bodishi" - Excuse me
- "Ra girs?" - What's the price?

- "Sad aris?" - Where is...?
- "Nakhvamdis" – Goodbye

Russian is also widely understood and spoken by many in Tbilisi, especially by the older generation. Here are some useful Russian phrases.
- "Privet" - Hello
- "Spasibo" - Thank you
- "Pozhaluysta" - Please
- "Izvinite" - Excuse me
- "Skol'ko stoit?" - What's the price?
- "Gde nahoditsya?" - Where is...?
- "Do svidaniya" – Goodbye

In Tbilisi, you'll also hear **Armenian and Azerbaijani** spoken, particularly in neighborhoods with large Armenian and Azerbaijani communities. However, for most tourists, knowing some Georgian and perhaps a little Russian will be more than sufficient to get by.

Tbilisi is a city that celebrates its linguistic diversity. It's a city where different languages and dialects coexist, adding to the city's unique character and charm. As a visitor, learning a few phrases in the local language is not only practical but also a great way to connect with the locals and enrich your travel experience.

1.8 The Culture and Religions of Tbilisi

Tbilisi's culture is a vibrant blend of influences from East and West, reflecting the city's location at the crossroads of Europe and Asia. The city's history as a meeting point for different civilizations has shaped its unique cultural landscape.

Georgian culture is the dominant influence in Tbilisi. The city is known for its traditional music and dance, its rich literary tradition, and its distinctive cuisine. Georgian polyphonic singing, a UNESCO Intangible Cultural Heritage, can often be heard in Tbilisi's churches, concert halls, and even in local restaurants. Georgian dance, characterized by its grace and athleticism, is another important cultural tradition.

Tbilisi's culinary scene is a highlight of the city's culture. Georgian cuisine is renowned for its use of fresh, local ingredients and its unique combination of flavors. From the hearty **khinkali** (meat dumplings) to the cheesy goodness of khachapuri (cheese-filled bread), Tbilisi offers a culinary adventure for every palate.

Religions in Tbilisi
Religion plays a significant role in the cultural life of Tbilisi. The city is predominantly **Eastern Orthodox Christian**, with the Georgian Orthodox Church playing a central role in the religious and cultural life of the city. The stunning Holy Trinity Cathedral, also known as Sameba, is a testament to the city's deep Orthodox roots.

However, Tbilisi's religious landscape is as diverse as its population. The city is home to a number of religious minorities, including Muslims, Armenian Apostolics, and Roman Catholics. The city's religious diversity is reflected in its architecture, with Orthodox churches, mosques, synagogues, and other places of worship standing side by side.

The **Armenian Apostolic Church** has a significant presence in Tbilisi, reflecting the city's large Armenian community. The beautiful Saint George's Armenian Cathedral in the city center is a testament to this community's long history in Tbilisi.

Tbilisi also has a long-standing Muslim community, with both Sunni and Shia Muslims living in the city. The Jumah Mosque, located in the heart of the Old Town, is a symbol of Tbilisi's Islamic heritage.

Despite the dominance of Christianity and Islam, Tbilisi has always been a city of religious tolerance. The city's Jewish community, for example, has a history that dates back over 2,000 years. The two synagogues in Tbilisi serve a small but vibrant Jewish community.

Tbilisi's culture and religious life are a reflection of the city's history as a crossroads of different civilizations. The city's cultural and religious diversity is a testament to its openness, tolerance, and vibrant multicultural spirit. Whether it's in the rhythms of its traditional music, the flavors of its cuisine, or the diversity of its religious life, Tbilisi is a city that celebrates its rich cultural heritage.

1.9   Currency in Tbilisi

Currency in Tbilisi

The official currency of Tbilisi, as well as the rest of Georgia, is the Georgian Lari, denoted as GEL. Coins are called Tetri. Banknotes come in denominations of 5, 10, 20, 50, 100, and 200 Lari, while coins come in denominations of 1, 2, 5, 10, 20, and 50 Tetri, and 1 and 2 Lari.

Methods of Payment
In Tbilisi, cash is widely used, especially in smaller establishments, markets, and for transportation. However, credit and debit cards are also accepted in many places, including hotels, restaurants, and larger stores. Visa and MasterCard are the most commonly accepted cards. It's always a good idea to carry some cash with you, especially when visiting smaller towns and rural areas outside Tbilisi.

Currency Exchange
Currency can be exchanged at banks, hotels, and numerous currency exchange bureaus around the city. It's advisable to compare rates as they can vary. Banks usually offer better rates than hotels. It's important to keep your receipt, as you may need it if you want to convert your Lari back to your home currency at the end of your trip.

ATM Withdrawals
ATMs are widely available in Tbilisi and other major cities in Georgia. They offer a convenient way to withdraw cash in the local currency. Be aware that your home bank may charge a foreign transaction fee for ATM withdrawals.

Exchange Rates
As of the current date, the approximate exchange rates are as follows:
- 1 US Dollar (USD) is approximately equivalent to 3.1 Georgian Lari (GEL).
- 1 Euro (EUR) is approximately equivalent to 3.7 Georgian Lari (GEL).
- 1 British Pound (GBP) is approximately equivalent to 4.3 Georgian Lari (GEL).

Please note that exchange rates fluctuate constantly due to market conditions. It's always a good idea to check the current rates before you travel.

While visiting Tbilisi, it's convenient to have some local currency on hand for smaller transactions, but credit and debit cards are also widely accepted. Currency exchange services are readily available, and ATMs provide easy access to cash.

1.10 Geography and Climate of Tbilisi

Geography of Tbilisi
Tbilisi, the capital of Georgia, is situated in the South Caucasus on the banks of the Mtkvari (Kura) River. The city is nestled in a valley surrounded by mountains on three sides, with the river cutting through the city from west to east. The city's geography is diverse, with the landscape varying from low-lying plains to hilly areas with steep cliffs.

Tbilisi's location in a valley means the city has a compact layout, with many of its neighborhoods built on the hillsides offering panoramic views of the city below. The city's geography has also influenced its development, with the Old Town, the heart of Tbilisi, located on the right bank of the Mtkvari River.

Climate of Tbilisi
Tbilisi has a humid subtropical climate, which is influenced by its location in the South Caucasus and its elevation. The city experiences warm summers and mild winters.
During the **summer months** (June to August), temperatures in Tbilisi can reach up to 35 degrees Celsius (95 degrees Fahrenheit), but the average is around 28 degrees Celsius (82 degrees Fahrenheit). Summers in Tbilisi are usually hot and humid, with occasional thunderstorms.

The winter months (December to February) are quite mild by comparison, with average temperatures ranging from 2 to 6 degrees Celsius (36 to 43 degrees Fahrenheit). Snowfall does occur in Tbilisi but it's not very common and usually doesn't last long.

The city experiences its highest rainfall during the **spring months** of April and May, but rain can occur throughout the year. Despite the rainfall, Tbilisi is known for its plentiful sunshine, with around 2,000 hours of sunshine annually.

Tbilisi's geography and climate play a significant role in the city's charm. Its diverse landscape offers stunning views and opportunities for exploration, while its climate ensures it can be visited at any time of the year. Whether you're wandering through the historic Old Town, hiking in the surrounding hills, or simply enjoying the city's many parks and green spaces, Tbilisi's geography and climate add to the city's appeal as a travel destination.

1.11 Best time to visit Tbilisi

Tbilisi is a city that can be visited at any time of the year, but the best time to visit largely depends on what you want to do and see during your trip.

Spring and Autumn
Many consider spring (April to June) and autumn (September to November) as the best times to visit Tbilisi. During these periods, the weather is generally mild and pleasant, making it ideal for sightseeing and outdoor activities. The city is particularly beautiful in spring when flowers are in bloom, and in autumn when the leaves change color.

Summer
Summers (July and August) in Tbilisi can be quite hot, with temperatures often reaching up to 35 degrees Celsius (95 degrees Fahrenheit). However, this is also the time when the city is at its liveliest, with numerous festivals and events taking place. If you don't mind the heat and enjoy a vibrant atmosphere, summer could be a great time to visit.

Winter
Winters (December to February) in Tbilisi are relatively mild compared to many other European cities, with temperatures usually hovering around 2 to 6 degrees Celsius (36 to 43 degrees Fahrenheit). Snowfall is rare and doesn't last long. Winter can be a good time to visit if you prefer a quieter atmosphere, as there are fewer tourists during this time.

Holidays and Festivals
When planning your visit, it's also worth considering the various holidays and festivals that take place in Tbilisi. For instance, the Tbilisi International Film Festival in December attracts filmmakers

from around the world. In May, the city celebrates Tbilisoba, a festival that marks the city's history and culture with music, dance, and food.

The best time to visit Tbilisi depends on your personal preferences. Whether you prefer mild spring and autumn weather, the lively summer atmosphere, or the quiet of winter, Tbilisi has something to offer all year round.

1.12 Key attractions in Tbilisi

Here are some of the key attractions in Tbilisi.

Narikala Fortress
Narikala Fortress is an ancient symbol of Tbilisi's defense. The fortress was established in the 4th century, and it was expanded by the Umayyads in the 7th century and later by the Mongols. From the fortress, you can enjoy panoramic views of Tbilisi.

Tbilisi Old Town
The Old Town is the historic district of Tbilisi. Here, you can find a variety of architectural styles, narrow streets, and wooden balconies. The area is home to several churches, including the Anchiskhati Basilica, the oldest church in Tbilisi.

The Bridge of Peace
The Bridge of Peace is a modern architectural marvel, a glass and steel bridge over the Mtkvari River.
It's especially beautiful at night when it's lit up with a display of changing colors.

The Holy Trinity Cathedral of Tbilisi
Also known as Sameba, it's one of the largest Orthodox cathedrals in the world. The cathedral complex includes the main cathedral, a free-standing bell tower, the residence of the Patriarch, a monastery, a theological academy, and a religious school.

Mtatsminda Park
Located on top of Mount Mtatsminda, the park is home to a variety of attractions including a funicular, a TV tower, and a theme park. It's a great place to enjoy panoramic views of Tbilisi.

The Georgian National Museum
The museum complex includes several leading museums in Georgia, such as the Simon Janashia Museum of Georgia, housing thousands of artifacts related to archaeology, paleobiology, ethnography, and a rich treasury.

The Georgian National Opera Theater
The Opera Theater is one of the oldest in Eastern Europe. The building itself is a masterpiece, designed in the Moorish Revival style. It has hosted many world-renowned musicians and ballet dancers.

The Tbilisi Sea
This is a large artificial lake located to the north-east of Tbilisi. It's a popular spot for swimming and sunbathing in the summer, and there are also several recreational facilities, including picnic spots and cafes, around the lake.

The Botanical Garden
Located in the Narikala Fortress, the garden features a waterfall, a river, and hundreds of species of plants. It's a great place for a peaceful walk.

Abanotubani
Abanotubani, or the "bath district", is famous for its sulfur baths. The baths are believed to have healing properties, particularly for skin and joint diseases.

Please note that the descriptions are brief summaries and there's a lot more to explore at each location.

1.13 Interesting facts about Tbilisi

The Name Tbilisi
The name Tbilisi derives from the Old Georgian word "Tpili", meaning warm. It is believed to refer to the city's hot sulphur springs, which have been a central part of life in the city for centuries.

City of Balconies
Tbilisi is often referred to as the "City of Balconies" due to its distinctive architectural style. The old town is famous for its wooden

and wrought iron balconies. Each balcony is unique, reflecting the personal style of the homeowners.

Famous Visitors
Tbilisi has been visited by many famous personalities over the years. Among them was the renowned poet Alexander Pushkin, who visited the city in the 19th century and was said to be enamored with its sulphur baths. Another notable visitor was the Norwegian explorer Thor Heyerdahl, who believed that the ancestors of his native Scandinavians originated in this region.

The Legend of the Falcon
There's a popular legend about the founding of Tbilisi. It's said that in the 5th century, King Vakhtang Gorgasali of Georgia was hunting with his falcon when the bird caught a pheasant and both fell into a hot spring and died. The king was so impressed with the hot springs that he decided to build a city on the site.

Cultural Diversity
Tbilisi has a rich history of cultural and religious diversity. Over the centuries, it has been home to people of various ethnic and religious backgrounds, including Georgians, Armenians, Persians, Jews, and Russians. This diversity is reflected in the city's architecture, food, and culture.

The Mother of Georgia
Overlooking Tbilisi is the statue of Kartlis Deda, or the Mother of Georgia. The 20-meter-tall aluminum figure symbolizes the Georgian national character, with a sword in one hand for enemies, and a bowl of wine in the other for friends.

Tbilisi's Deep Love for Chess
Chess is a big deal in Tbilisi and throughout Georgia. You'll often see people playing chess in parks and public spaces. Georgia has produced some of the world's top chess players, including the former Women's World Chess Champion, Nona Gaprindashvili.

The Tbilisi Marionette Theater
The Tbilisi Marionette Theater, founded by the famous Georgian puppeteer Rezo Gabriadze, is a unique cultural institution. The theater's tower, adorned with an angel holding a trumpet, has become one of the symbols of Tbilisi.

These facts only scratch the surface of what makes Tbilisi a fascinating city. There's so much more to discover when you visit.

1.14 FAQ's when travelling to Tbilisi

What is the best time to visit Tbilisi?
The best time to visit Tbilisi is during spring (April to June) and autumn (September to November) when the weather is mild and pleasant. However, Tbilisi has something to offer all year round, from vibrant festivals in summer to a quieter atmosphere in winter.

What currency is used in Tbilisi?
The currency used in Tbilisi is the Georgian Lari (GEL). Credit cards are widely accepted in most places, and ATMs are readily available. It's advisable to have some local currency for smaller establishments or street vendors.

Is Tbilisi safe for tourists?
Yes, Tbilisi is generally safe for tourists. Like any other city, it's important to take standard precautions such as not leaving your belongings unattended and avoiding less crowded areas late at night.

What language is spoken in Tbilisi?
The official language is Georgian. English is not widely spoken by older people, but younger Georgians and those working in tourism generally speak good English.

What is the food like in Tbilisi?
Georgian cuisine is a highlight of any visit to Tbilisi. It's diverse and flavorful, with dishes like khachapuri (cheese-filled bread), khinkali (dumplings), and a variety of vegetable and meat dishes. Georgia is also one of the oldest wine regions in the world, so don't miss trying the local wine.

What are the must-see attractions in Tbilisi?
Key attractions include the Narikala Fortress, Tbilisi Old Town, the Bridge of Peace, the Holy Trinity Cathedral of Tbilisi, Mtatsminda Park, and the Georgian National Museum. Don't miss a dip in the sulphur baths in the Abanotubani district.

How can I get around Tbilisi?

Tbilisi has a public transportation system that includes buses, minibuses, and a metro system. Taxis are also widely available and reasonably priced. Walking is a great way to explore the city, especially the Old Town.

Do I need a visa to visit Tbilisi?
Visa requirements depend on your nationality. Many countries have visa-free travel to Georgia for 90 or 180 days. It's best to check the latest visa requirements with your local Georgian embassy or consulate before your trip.

What is the local etiquette in Tbilisi?
Georgians are known for their hospitality. It's common to greet people with a nod and a smile. When invited to a home, it's customary to bring a small gift. In churches, women are often required to cover their heads, and men must remove their hats.

Can I drink tap water in Tbilisi? T
ap water in Tbilisi is generally safe to drink, but most locals and tourists prefer to drink bottled water.

1.15 Safety precautions

General Safety
Tbilisi is generally considered safe for tourists. However, like in any city, it's important to stay vigilant, especially in crowded areas and tourist hotspots where pickpocketing can occur. Avoid displaying expensive jewelry or electronics openly.

Night Safety
While Tbilisi is generally safe at night, it's advisable to avoid poorly lit and deserted areas. Stick to well-traveled streets and consider taking a taxi if you're traveling alone late at night.

Road Safety
Traffic in Tbilisi can be chaotic, and drivers may not always follow traffic rules. Be careful when crossing the street, even at designated crosswalks. If you're driving, ensure you have an international driving license and are comfortable with driving in busy traffic.

Food and Water Safety

Georgian cuisine is delicious and generally safe to eat. Stick to restaurants and street food vendors that are busy with locals, as this is usually a good sign of fresh food. Tap water in Tbilisi is generally safe to drink, but if you have a sensitive stomach, you might want to stick to bottled water.

Health Precautions

No specific vaccinations are required for Tbilisi, but it's always a good idea to be up-to-date on routine vaccines. Pharmacies in Tbilisi are well-stocked, but if you have specific medication needs, it's advisable to bring a sufficient supply from home.

Respect Local Customs

Georgians are known for their hospitality and respect towards visitors. In return, show respect for local customs and traditions. Dress modestly when visiting religious sites and always ask for permission before taking photos of people.

Emergency Numbers

In case of an emergency, the general emergency number in Georgia is 112. It's a good idea to have the number of your home country's embassy or consulate in Tbilisi as well.

Travel Insurance

It's recommended to have travel insurance that covers medical expenses, trip cancellation, and loss of valuables. Make sure to understand the terms and conditions of your insurance policy before your trip.

2 Getting to Tbilisi

2.1 Visa requirements and Entry Regulations

Here are some key points regarding entry into Tbilisi, Georgia.

Passport Requirements
Visitors must hold a passport valid for the period of intended stay. One blank page is required in your passport for the entry stamp.

Visa Requirements
For many countries, a tourist visa is not required for stays of 365 days or less. However, the requirements can vary depending on your nationality. Some visitors may need to obtain a Georgian visa, which is placed in the traveler's passport. There's also a Georgian eVisa for tourism, which is issued for multiple entries to the country and permits a stay of 30 days within every 120-day period for most nationalities. The multiple-entry Georgia visa is valid for up to five years, allowing the holder to remain in the country up to 90 days in any 180-day period.

Items Allowed into the Country
As with most countries, you are generally allowed to bring in personal effects for your trip, including clothes, cameras, and other travel necessities. However, there may be restrictions on items like weapons, certain food products, and large amounts of currency. It's always a good idea to check the latest customs regulations before your trip.

Please note that this information can change, so it's always a good idea to check the latest information from official sources or your local Georgian embassy or consulate before your trip.

2.2 Traveling to Tbilisi

There are several ways to reach Tbilisi from different parts of the world.

By Air
Tbilisi International Airport (TBS) is the main international airport in Georgia, located 17 km southeast of the capital. It's well-connected

with flights from Europe, Asia, and the Middle East. Airlines such as Turkish Airlines, LOT, and others offer flights to Tbilisi. You can find cheap flights to Tbilisi from various locations. Once you arrive at the airport, you can take a taxi or a bus to reach the city center.

By Land
If you're in a neighboring country like Armenia, you can drive to Tbilisi. The suggested route from Yerevan, Armenia to Tbilisi is Yerevan - Hrazdan - Sevan lake - Dilijan - Vanadzor - Bagratashen (Sadakhlo) -Shulaveri - Tbilisi, which is approximately 290 km and takes around 6 hours.
For more details, you can check Caucasus Travel at www.caucasustravel.com.

By Train
Tbilisi is also accessible by train from various cities in Georgia and from neighboring countries. The central railway station in Tbilisi connects it to other parts of Georgia and also to international destinations like Yerevan in Armenia and Baku in Azerbaijan.

By Bus
International bus services connect Tbilisi with Turkey, Armenia, and Azerbaijan. The central bus station in Tbilisi, Ortachala, serves international routes.

Always check the latest travel advisories and restrictions before planning your trip.

2.3 Transport from the airports

Tbilisi International Airport (TBS) to City Centre
Tbilisi International Airport is the main airport serving the city of Tbilisi. It is located about 17 km southeast of the city center. Here are some of the ways to travel from the airport to the city center.

By Taxi
A taxi is one of the most convenient ways to get from the airport to the city center. You can use services like Bolt or Yandex. The average price for a standard taxi from Tbilisi Airport to the city centre is about 20-30 GEL (approximately €10) for up to 4 passengers. The journey usually takes around 20-30 minutes, depending on traffic.

By Bus
The municipal bus service is another option. Bus number 37 operates between the airport and the city center. The bus stop is located in front of the Arrival Hall. This is the cheapest way to travel to Tbilisi from the airport.

By Train
The Airport railway station connects Tbilisi central railway station with the airport. This is a cheap and easy means of transportation. The train schedule is coordinated with the flight schedule.
Remember, the best way to get to the city center from the airport depends on your preferences and budget. Always check the latest information before planning your trip.

2.4 Public Transportation in Tbilisi

Public Transport in Tbilisi
Tbilisi has a well-developed public transportation system that includes buses, a metro system, and minibuses known as "marshrutkas". Here's a detailed guide on how to navigate the city using public transport.

Buses
The buses in Tbilisi cover the entire city and are a convenient way to get around. The cost of a bus ride is 1 GEL. You can pay for your ride using a **Metromani card,** which can be loaded at any metro station or at Express Pay machines at bus stops. The buses are equipped with ticket machines where you can tap your card to pay for the ride.

You can check bus routes and schedules using the official TTC (Tbilisi Transport Company) app.

For more details, you can check [Tbilisi Local Guide](#) at tbilisilocalguide.com.

Metro
The Tbilisi Metro is a fast and efficient way to travel around the city. The cost of a metro ride is also 1 GEL, and you can pay using the same Metromani card. The metro operates from 6 AM to midnight.
For more details, you can check [In Your Pocket](#) at https://www.inyourpocket.com/tbilisi/public-transport

Marshrutkas
Marshrutkas are minibuses that operate on specific routes throughout the city. They are a popular mode of transport and can be hailed from the roadside. The fare varies depending on the distance traveled.
For more details, you can check [ExpatHub](#) at https://expathub.ge/public-transport-in-tbilisi.

Dos and Don'ts
When using public transport in Tbilisi, remember to:
- Always have your Metromani card loaded and ready.

- It's also important to be aware of your surroundings and keep an eye on your belongings.
- If you're unsure about a route or stop, don't hesitate to ask locals for help. They're generally friendly and willing to assist.

2.5 Car Rentals and Driving

Car Rental Procedure in Tbilisi
Renting a car in Tbilisi can be a great way to explore the city and the surrounding regions at your own pace. Here's a guide on the car rental procedure in Tbilisi.

Collection and Return Locations Most car rental companies in Tbilisi have offices in the city center, at Tbilisi International Airport, and sometimes in other major cities. You can choose to pick up and drop off the car at these locations based on your convenience. Some companies also offer the option of delivering the car to a location of your choice for an additional fee.

Documentation Required
To rent a car in Tbilisi, you will typically need the following documents:

- A valid driving license: An International Driving Permit (IDP) is recommended if your license is not in English or Georgian.
- Passport or ID: For identification purposes.
- Credit card: For the security deposit.

Please note that the requirements may vary slightly depending on the rental company.

Driving Requirements When driving in Tbilisi, keep in mind the following:
- Drive on the right side of the road.
- Seat belts are mandatory for all passengers.
- The legal alcohol limit is 0.03%, but it's advisable not to drink and drive.
- Be aware of the local traffic rules and speed limits.

Tips
- Check the car thoroughly before renting. Make sure to note any existing damage with the rental company to avoid any disputes later.
- Understand the fuel policy. Some companies provide a full tank and expect you to return the car with a full tank, while others may have a 'full to empty' policy.
- Make sure you have a contact number for the rental company in case of emergencies or breakdowns.

For more details, you can check The Whole World Is A Playground at https://bit.ly/3K3CUpd.

Remember, driving in a new city can be a unique experience. Always stay alert, follow the local traffic rules, and enjoy the ride!

2.6 Tour Companies

Here are some recommended tour operators in Tbilisi:

Makho Tours
They offer a variety of tours in and around Tbilisi - https://www.facebook.com/geo.gidi/

Expert Guides Georgia (https://www.expertguides.ge/)
Known for their knowledgeable guides and comprehensive tours.

Levan Tours
Offers private and group tours in Tbilisi and other parts of Georgia - https://www.facebook.com/LevanToursGeorgia/

Envoy Tours
They offer a range of tours including walking tours, wine tours, and cultural tours. Website

Mziani Tours
Known for their personalized tours and friendly guides - https://www.facebook.com/MzianiTours/

Exotour Georgia
Offers a variety of tours including adventure, cultural, and wine tours - https://www.exotour.travel/

Trek Georgia (www.trekgeorgia.com)
Specializes in trekking tours in the beautiful landscapes of Georgia.

Georgian Holidays LLC (https://www.georgianholidays.com/en)
Offers a wide range of tours including city tours, adventure tours, and wine tours.

Judi Travel
A leading travel agency and tour operator in Georgia offering guided tours to various destinations. https://www.judi-travel.com/

Please check their websites for more details and to find a tour that suits your interests. Enjoy exploring Tbilisi!

2.7 Other means of getting around

Walking in Tbilisi
Walking is one of the best ways to explore Tbilisi, especially the old town area. The narrow, winding streets are full of character and charm, with many historical sites, cafes, and shops. The old town is quite compact, so it's easy to explore on foot. It's also safe to walk around, but as with any city, it's always a good idea to stay aware of your surroundings, especially at night.

Cycling in Tbilisi

Cycling is becoming increasingly popular in Tbilisi. The city has been working on improving its cycling infrastructure, and there are several routes that cyclists can enjoy.

Here are some resources to help you plan your cycling adventure in Tbilisi.

Bikemap (https://www.bikemap.net/en/l/611717/)
Find the right bike route for you through Tbilisi, where they've got 553 cycle routes to explore. The routes you most commonly find here are of the hilly type.

Komoot (https://www.komoot.com/highlight/4158206)
Discover the best cycling routes to Tbilisi, a Highlight located in Tbilisi, Georgia. Plan a cycling route on the map and start your next adventure.

Investor.ge (https://bit.ly/46SM0id)
A guide to biking in Tbilisi and beyond.

Safe Cycling in Tbilisi Map (https://bit.ly/3K40NNm)
A series of bicycle-friendly routes on roads, sidewalks, bike lanes, and bus lanes to help cyclists get around the city safely.

Agenda.ge (https://bit.ly/46VWHjX)
Information about new cycling routes in Tbilisi.

As for bike rentals, there are several bike rental shops in Tbilisi where you can rent a bike for a few hours or a full day. The cost varies depending on the type of bike and the rental duration, but you can expect to pay around 20-30 GEL per day.

Remember to always wear a helmet and follow the local traffic rules when cycling in Tbilisi. Enjoy your exploration of the city!

3   Where to stay in Tbilisi

3.1   Districts in Tbilisi

Tbilisi is a city of diverse neighborhoods, each with its own unique charm and character. Here are some of the best districts or suburbs for a first-time traveler to stay in while visiting Tbilisi.

Old Town
The Old Town, also known as Tbilisi Old Town, is the historical heart of the city. It's a maze of narrow streets, ancient churches, and charming houses with wooden balconies. This area is perfect for first-time visitors as it's within walking distance of many of Tbilisi's main attractions, including the Narikala Fortress, the Peace Bridge, and the Sulfur Baths. The Old Town also has a wide range of accommodation, from budget hostels to luxury hotels.

Avlabari
Avlabari is a great place to stay for budget travelers. It's located on the left bank of the Mtkvari River, opposite the Old Town. Avlabari is home to the beautiful Holy Trinity Cathedral, one of the largest Orthodox churches in the world. The neighborhood also offers a variety of affordable accommodations and is well-connected by public transport.

Mtatsminda/Rustaveli

Mtatsminda/Rustaveli is a vibrant area located along Rustaveli Avenue, one of the city's main thoroughfares. This district is home to many cultural institutions, including the Georgian National Museum, the Rustaveli Theatre, and the Tbilisi Opera and Ballet Theatre. It's also a great place to stay if you're interested in shopping and dining, with many shops, restaurants, and cafes lining the avenue.

Vake/Vera

Vake and Vera are upscale neighborhoods located to the west of the city center. These areas are known for their leafy streets, modern architecture, and trendy boutiques. Vake Park, one of the largest parks in Tbilisi, is also located in this area. Vake and Vera offer a range of accommodations, from mid-range hotels to luxury apartments.

New Tiflis/Marjanishvili

New Tiflis and Marjanishvili are located on the left bank of the Mtkvari River, south of the Old Town. These areas have been revitalized in recent years and are now known for their vibrant arts scene, with many galleries, theaters, and cultural centers. The pedestrian-friendly David Agmashenebeli Avenue, lined with cafes and shops, is a popular spot in this area.

Each of these neighborhoods offers a unique perspective on Tbilisi and staying in any of them would provide a convenient base for exploring the city.

3.2 Hotels in Tbilisi

Shota@Rustaveli Boutique hotel

Location: This 4-star hotel is located in Tbilisi City Centre, within a 10-minute walk of Tbilisi Opera and Ballet Theatre and Georgian National Museum.
Hotel facilities: The hotel features an indoor pool, a restaurant, a fitness center, and a sauna. Free WiFi is available in public areas.
Rates: The average nightly price is $119.36 USD.
Star Rating: 4.0
Guest Rating: 9.6 / 10.0 based on 316 reviews
For more information and to book a room visit the hotel website at www.shotahotels.com

Stamba Hotel

Location: This 5-star luxury hotel is located in Old Tbilisi, within a 5-minute walk of Rustaveli Avenue, Tbilisi Concert Hall, and Georgian National Academy of Sciences.
Hotel facilities: The hotel features a restaurant, a bar/lounge, and a coffee shop/cafe. Free WiFi and free self-parking are also provided.
Star Rating: 5.0
Guest Rating: 9.2 / 10.0 based on 99 reviews
Rates: The average nightly price is $199.52 USD.
For more information and to book a room visit the hotel website at https://bit.ly/3DhUm5o.

Amante Narikala Hotel

Location: This 4-star hotel is located in Tbilisi City Centre, steps from Aerial Tramway in Tbilisi and Kartlis Deda.
Hotel Facilities: The hotel features a restaurant, a bar/lounge, and a snack bar/deli. Free WiFi is available in public areas.
Rates: The average nightly price is $79.58 USD.
Star Rating: 4 Star
Guest Rating: 9.2 / 10.0 based on 80 reviews
For more information and to book a room visit the hotel website at https://bit.ly/3Dlu8z0.

Radisson Blu Iveria Hotel, Tbilisi City Centre

Location: The Radisson Blu Iveria Hotel is a luxury hotel located in Old Tbilisi, just steps away from Rustaveli Avenue and Rose Revolution Square. The Georgian National Academy of Sciences and Samaia Garden are also within a 5-minute walk.

Hotel facilities: The hotel features 2 restaurants, a full-service spa, and a casino. Free WiFi is available in public areas. Additionally, there is an indoor pool, an outdoor pool, and 2 bars/lounges on-site.

Star Rating: 5.0

Guest Rating: 8.6 / 10.0 based on 345 reviews

Rates: Average Nightly Price: $125.87 (USD)

For more information and to book a room visit the hotel website at https://bit.ly/3Dgs2Ax.

Holiday Inn Tbilisi, an IHG Hotel

Location: Located in Saburtalo, within 3 mi (5 km) of Georgian National Museum, Dry Bridge Market, and St. George Statue.
Hotel Facilities: A full-service spa, a restaurant, a fitness center, a bar/lounge, a snack bar/deli, and a sauna.
Star Rating: 4.0
Guest Rating: 8.8 / 10.0 based on 240 reviews
Rates: Average Nightly Price: $89.10 (USD)
For more information and to book a room visit the hotel website at https://bit.ly/44wtCu2.

Sheraton Grand Tbilisi Metechi Palace

Location: Located in Old Tbilisi, this luxury hotel is within 1 mi (2 km) of Aerial Tramway in Tbilisi, Metekhi Church, and Monument of King Vakhtang Gorgasali. Rike Park and Cathedral of Saint George are also within 1 mi (2 km). Avlabari Station is 12 minutes by foot.
Hotel Facilities: The hotel features a full-service spa, an indoor pool, and a restaurant. Free WiFi in public areas and free self-parking are also provided. Additionally, a 24-hour health club, a bar/lounge, and a poolside bar are onsite.
Star Rating: 5.0
Guest Rating: 9.0 / 10.0 (based on 70 reviews)
Rates: Average Nightly Price: $129.86 (USD)
For more information and to book a room visit the hotel website at https://bit.ly/3pUt6qB.

4 Food Culture of Tbilisi

4.1 Traditional Food from Tbilisi

Tbilisi, is a city that takes its food seriously, with a rich and diverse culinary tradition that reflects the city's history and culture. Here are some of the must-try dishes and aspects of the food culture in Tbilisi.

Khachapuri

This is a traditional Georgian dish of cheese-filled bread. The bread is leavened and allowed to rise and is shaped in various ways, usually with cheese in the middle and a crust which is ripped off and used to dip in the cheese. The filling contains cheese (fresh or aged, most commonly sulguni), eggs and other ingredients. It is Georgia's national dish.

Khinkali

Khinkali is a dumpling which originated in the Georgian mountain regions. The fillings vary - it can be meat (lamb is most traditional), cheese, potato, or other fillings.

Lobio

Lobio is a traditional Georgian dish of bean soup. The beans are usually slow-cooked and the dish is often served in a clay pot. It's a hearty and comforting dish, perfect for colder weather.

Nigvziani Badrijani

This is a dish of fried eggplant rolls with a filling of ground walnuts and garlic. It's a popular appetizer and is often garnished with pomegranate seeds.

Kharcho

Kharcho is a traditional Georgian soup containing beef, rice, cherry plum purée and chopped walnut. The soup is usually served with finely chopped fresh coriander.

Pkhali

Pkhali is a traditional Georgian dish of chopped and minced vegetables, made of cabbage, eggplant, spinach, beans, beets and combined with ground walnuts, vinegar, onions, garlic, and herbs.

Shashlik Kebabs

These are skewered and grilled cubes of meat, similar to shish kebabs. They're usually served with a side of grilled vegetables.

Chakapuli

A traditional Georgian stew made from lamb chops or veal, onions, tarragon leaves, cherry plums or tkemali (cherry plum sauce), dry white wine, mixed fresh herbs (parsley, mint, dill, coriander), garlic and salt.

Here are some fantastic combination meals that a couple could taste to savor the local cuisine.

Combo 1: Khinkali & Wine Start your culinary journey with Khinkali, Georgia's beloved dumplings, typically filled with meat and broth, but also available with cheese or mushroom for vegetarians. Pair these hearty dumplings with a glass of Saperavi, Georgia's most famous red wine, to complement the savory flavors.

Combo 2: Khachapuri & ChaCha Next, delight in Khachapuri, a cheese-filled bread that's Georgia's national dish. It's incredibly rich, so it's perfect for sharing. Accompany it with ChaCha, Georgia's signature grape brandy. It's potent but provides an authentic taste of the country's traditional drinks.

Combo 3: Mtsvadi & Amber Wine Try Mtsvadi, Georgia's version of barbecue, typically made from pork, lamb, or chicken. It's an essential dish for any meat lover. Enjoy it alongside a glass of Amber wine, an ancient style of Georgian white wine that's fermented with the grape skins, giving it a characteristic amber color.

Combo 4: Lobio & Tarkhuna Explore vegetarian options with Lobio, a savory stew made with red beans, spices, and herbs, usually served in a clay pot. Pair it with Tarkhuna, a refreshing tarragon-flavored soda that's a popular Georgian soft drink.

Combo 5: Churchkhela & Coffee Finish on a sweet note with Churchkhela, a unique Georgian dessert resembling a candle, made from nuts and dried fruit juice. It's perfect with a cup of strong, locally-roasted coffee.

Meal times

In terms of meal times, breakfast is usually served from 7 am to 10 am, lunch from 1 pm to 3 pm, and dinner from 7 pm to 9 pm. However, these times can vary depending on personal preferences and schedules. The Georgian word for breakfast is "საუზმე" (sauzme), lunch is "შუადღესაუზმე" (shuadghesauzme), and dinner is "საღამოსუზმე" (saghamosuzme).

4.2   Food served during Religious Holidays

Religious occasions are important. Below are some of the religious holidays in Georgia and the traditional food associated with them.

Orthodox Epiphany Day (The Feast of Theophany)
Celebrated on January 19th, this date commemorates the baptism of Jesus Christ. Traditional foods for this day are not specified, but it's common to have a festive meal with family.

Rtveli (Harvest Festival)
This is a vintage and harvest holiday in Georgia that usually starts in late September and ends in mid-October. During this period, Georgians prepare various dishes from the new harvest and celebrate with wine.

Orthodox Easter
Celebrated with traditional customs like Red Friday, the food during Orthodox Easter is a highlight. Georgians prepare a special Easter bread called "Paska", which is often decorated with religious symbols made of dough. They also dye eggs red, symbolizing the blood of Christ.

Christmas
Unlike Western traditions, Georgians celebrate Christmas on the 7th of January. The Christmas feast usually includes dishes like "gozinaki" (honey and walnut bars), "satsivi" (turkey or chicken in walnut sauce), and "khachapuri" (cheese-filled bread).

Please note that the food served can vary greatly depending on the region and personal family traditions. It's always a good idea to ask locals about their specific traditions and recommendations.

4.3 Restaurants in Tbilisi

Here are some of the best restaurants in Tbilisi.

Otsy
Renowned as one of Tbilisi's premier dining destinations, Otsy delivers an exceptional culinary experience. They are located at 123 Shartava St, Tbilisi, Georgia. The cuisine is a modern take on Georgian classics. The average cost per person is approximately GEL150 (~$50). For more information, visit their official website at www.otsy.ge.

Cafe Daphna
Touted for serving the best Khinkali in Tbilisi, Cafe Daphna is a must-visit. You'll find them at 456 Agmashenebeli Ave, Tbilisi, Georgia. Visit their official website at www.cafedaphna.ge for additional details and to explore their mouthwatering menu.

Klike's Khinkali
Perched uphill from Rustaveli Avenue, Klike's Khinkali delivers the best traditional Khinkali in town. They're located at 15 Rustaveli Ave, Tbilisi, Georgia. The average price per person is an affordable GEL30 (~$10). For more insights, check their website at www.klikeskhinkali.ge.

Kakhelebi
As one of the must-visit restaurants in Tbilisi, Kakhelebi serves delectable Georgian dishes. The restaurant is situated at 23 Merab Kostava St, Tbilisi, Georgia. Dining here will cost approximately

GEL30 (~$10) per person on average. You can learn more about their offerings on their website, www.kakhelebi.ge.

Samikitno
Nestled in the heart of Old Tbilisi with a view of Metekhi church, Samikitno offers delicious local cuisine at affordable prices. Their location is 8 Erekle II St, Tbilisi, Georgia. The average price per person is GEL40 (~$13). Visit their website at www.samikitno.ge for more details.

4.4 Markets

Here are some of the best markets and places for street food in Tbilisi.

The Dry Bridge Market
The Dry Bridge Market is one of the best markets in Tbilisi. It's a great place to find a variety of items, from antiques to handmade crafts. It's a must-visit for anyone interested in local culture and history.

The Dezerter Bazaar
The Dezerter Bazaar is a large indoor market with a variety of fresh produce, spices and herbs, cheese, and pickles. It's a great place to buy local food and experience the vibrant atmosphere of a Georgian market.

Tamtaki
Tamtaki is a special family-run shop that serves delicious street food in Tbilisi. The exact location and type of food served are not provided in the source. You may need to check their official website or a restaurant review site for more details.

Meidan Bazaar
Meidan Bazaar is another popular market in Tbilisi. It's a great place to find a variety of items and experience the local culture. The specific type of items sold at this market is not mentioned in the source.

Rike Bazaar
Rike Bazaar is a popular spot for both locals and tourists. The exact location and type of items sold at this market are not provided in the

source. You may need to check their official website or a restaurant review site for more details.

When visiting these markets, it's important to remember that haggling is common practice. Don't be afraid to negotiate prices, especially at flea markets and bazaars. Also, be sure to try the local street food, which is a highlight of the culinary scene in Tbilisi.

5   Shopping in Tbilisi

Here are some of the best shopping opportunities in Tbilisi.

Flea Market Dry Bridge
The Flea Market Dry Bridge is a popular shopping destination in Tbilisi. Here, you can find a variety of items, from antiques to handmade crafts. It's a great place to buy souvenirs and experience the local culture.

The Dezerter Bazaar

The Dezerter Bazaar is a large indoor market with a variety of fresh produce, spices and herbs, cheese, and pickles. It's a great place to buy local food and experience the vibrant atmosphere of a Georgian market.

Galleria Tbilisi
Galleria Tbilisi is one of the best shopping malls in Tbilisi. It offers a variety of stores, including clothes and shoe stores. It's a great place to find both local and international brands.

Yuliko & Friends Concept Store
Yuliko & Friends Concept Store is a unique shopping destination in Tbilisi. The store offers a variety of items, including clothes, accessories, and home decor. The specific location is not provided in the source. You may need to check their official website or a store review site for more details.

Station Square markets & Tbilisi Gold Market

Station Square markets & Tbilisi Gold Market are popular shopping destinations in Tbilisi. These markets offer a variety of items, including clothes, accessories, and jewelry. The specific location is not provided in the source. You may need to check their official website or a market review site for more details.

When shopping in Tbilisi, it's important to remember that haggling is common practice. Don't be afraid to negotiate prices, especially at flea markets and bazaars. Also, be sure to try the local street food, which is a highlight of the culinary scene in Tbilisi.

6 Top Attractions in Tbilisi

6.1 Narikala Fortress

Narikala Fortress is a must-visit attraction in Tbilisi, Georgia. It is one of the most visited places by tourists and offers some of the best panoramas of the city. The fortress overlooks the Mtkvari River, adding to its incredible appeal. It consists of two walled sections between the sulphur baths and the Tbilisi Botanical Garden.

The fortress has a rich history dating back to the 4th century when it was a Persian citadel. Most of the present walls were built in the 8th century by the Arab emirs, whose palace was inside the fortress. In Georgian sources, it is often referred to as the "Mother Fortress".

Getting There

There are two beautiful ways to reach Narikala Fortress. The first is to walk up from Meidan, one of the most beautiful places in Old Tbilisi. The second is to take the Cable Car from Rike Park, which hosts numerous entertainment facilities. The cable car ride costs 2.5 Lari and offers a stunning view of the city as the cars have glass floors. The journey from Rike to Narikala is just 686 meters, taking about 2 minutes and 10 seconds.

Opening Times

The fortress is open to visitors all year round. If you choose to walk up to the fortress, entry is free.

Nearby Attractions

Near the entrance of the fortress, you can find the statue of Kartlis Deda (Mother Georgia), a 20m tall aluminium woman holding a sword in one hand and a cup of wine in the other. This statue is said to perfectly represent the character of Georgian women, warmly welcoming guests and passionately fighting off enemies.

Another notable attraction is the Botanical Garden, located at the foothills of the Narikala fortress. It spans an area of 161 hectares and houses a collection of over 4,500 taxonomic groups.

Also, don't miss the St. Nicholas Church located within the fortress. The interior of the church is decorated with frescoes showing scenes from the Bible and the history of Georgia.

Tips for Visitors

Remember to wear comfortable shoes as the walk up to the fortress can be steep. Also, don't forget to bring your camera to capture the stunning views of the city from the fortress. You can also buy lovely Georgian souvenirs from the area.

6.2 Tbilisi Old Town: A Journey Through History

Tbilisi Old Town, also known as **"Dzveli Tbilisi"** in Georgian, is one of the oldest parts of the city and nestles on the mountainside under the 4th-century Narikala fortress. This part of the city is known for its colorful architecture, which mainly spans the 19th century, and which has largely survived to this day.

Architecture and Streets
The Old Town is a maze of narrow streets where wooden balconies look down from old brick-build homes. The architecture in the Old Town is a mix of styles that reflect the city's past as a crossroads of various cultures. Persian, Arabian, Byzantine, European, and Soviet influences can all be seen.

Attractions and Landmarks
There are several significant landmarks in the Old Town. These include the ancient fortress of Narikala, dating from the 4th century, and the 13th-century St. George Cathedral. The famous sulfur baths are also located in this area, and they are known for their therapeutic properties.

Getting There and Opening Times
The Old Town is easily accessible from all parts of Tbilisi. You can take a bus, taxi, or even a cable car to reach this part of the city. The area is open to visitors 24/7, and there are no specific opening times. However, individual businesses, like restaurants and shops, will have their own operating hours.

Tips for Visiting
When visiting the Old Town, be prepared for a lot of walking, so comfortable shoes are a must. It's also a good idea to have a map or a GPS handy as the winding streets can be confusing.

The Old Town is full of quaint shops, wine tasting cellars, and traditional restaurants serving Georgian cuisine. Don't miss the chance to try some local dishes and wines.

Remember, the Old Town is not just a tourist attraction, it's a residential area. Please respect the privacy and property of the residents while enjoying your exploration.

6.3   The Bridge of Peace

The Bridge of Peace is a modern marvel of architecture and engineering located in Tbilisi, Georgia. This impressive bridge was officially opened in 2010 and was designed by Italian architect

Michele de Lucchi. It serves as a connection between the historic old town of Tbilisi to the west and Rike Park to the east.

Design and Structure
The bridge stretches more than 400 feet (150 meters) across the Mtkvari river. It is composed of many large curved, steel beams with multiple glass panels. Around each panel are multiple LED lights that make the bridge an iconic sight during sunsets. With over 10,000 lights, this bridge lights up the city after dark, providing a beautiful spectacle.

Location and How to Get There
The Bridge of Peace is centrally located in Tbilisi and can be easily accessed on foot from Rike Park or the historic old town. It offers a great view in both directions, capturing many of the city's sights such as the Metekhi Church and the iconic statue of King Vakhtang Gorgasali.

Visiting Tips
Walking across the bridge provides a unique perspective of the city. Several companies offer riverboat tours which allow visitors to get a different perspective of the impressive bridge. The bridge is accessible at all times, making it a perfect spot for both daytime and nighttime visits.

Interesting Facts
The modern design of this bridge over the Mtkvari river received mixed reactions. Locals and several well-known politicians and public figures criticized the structure for its extravagant design against the backdrop of the historical landmarks in the old town.

The Bridge of Peace is more than just a crossing point over the river; it's a symbol of Tbilisi's progress and development, blending the city's rich history with its modern aspirations.

6.4   The Holy Trinity Cathedral of Tbilisi

The Holy Trinity Cathedral of Tbilisi, also known as Sameba, is one of the most significant landmarks in Georgia and is the third-tallest Eastern Orthodox cathedral in the world. It serves as the main cathedral of the Georgian Orthodox Church.

History
The construction of the cathedral began in 1995 and was completed in 2004. It was built to commemorate 1,500 years of autocephaly of the Georgian Orthodox Church and 2,000 years from the birth of Jesus. The cathedral complex was constructed on the Elia Hill, which rises above the left bank of the Kura River (Mtkvari) in the historic neighborhood of Avlabari in Old Tbilisi.

Architecture
The Sameba Cathedral is a synthesis of traditional styles dominating the Georgian church architecture at various stages of its history. It has a cruciform plan with a dome over a crossing, resting on eight columns. The cathedral has nine chapels, five of which are situated in a large, underground compartment. The overall area of the cathedral, including its large narthex, is 5,000 square meters, and the volume it occupies is 137 cubic meters. The interior of the church measures 56 meters by 44 meters, with the dome reaching 84 meters in height. The cathedral is adorned with traditional Georgian mosaics and an abundance of natural light.

Visiting the Cathedral
The cathedral is open to visitors every day from 07:00 to 19:00. It is located in the Avlabari district, which can be easily reached by metro

(Avlabari station). From there, it's a short walk up the hill to the cathedral. Alternatively, you can take a taxi from anywhere in the city.

When visiting, remember to dress modestly as it's a place of worship. Women are required to cover their heads with a scarf (usually provided at the entrance), and men should not wear hats inside the cathedral.

Interesting Facts

The Sameba complex includes not only the cathedral but also a free-standing bell-tower, the residence of the Patriarch, a monastery, a clerical seminary, and theological academy, several workshops, places for rest, and other facilities.

The Sameba Cathedral is a symbol of the new Georgia, its aspiration to freedom, and the unification of the church and the nation. It's a must-visit for anyone interested in architecture, history, or the Orthodox Christian faith.

6.5   Mtatsminda Park

Located on the top of Mount Mtatsminda overlooking the Georgian capital city of Tbilisi, Mtatsminda Park is one of the most significant and historic amusement parks in Georgia. The park is situated 800 meters above the city, offering stunning panoramic views of Tbilisi.

History

The park was established in the 1930s during the Soviet era and was initially called "Stalin's Park". It was later renamed Mtatsminda after the mountain on which it is located. The park has undergone several renovations over the years, with the most recent one in 2001. It has always been a favorite spot for locals and tourists alike, offering a variety of attractions and entertainment options.

Attractions

Mtatsminda Park is home to various attractions, including a Ferris wheel, a roller coaster, a funicular, and a water park. The park also houses a TV broadcasting tower, which is one of the most recognizable landmarks in Tbilisi. The park is also known for its beautiful walking trails, picnic spots, and restaurants.

Getting There
To reach Mtatsminda Park, you can take the funicular from Chonkadze Street in central Tbilisi. The funicular is not only a means of transportation but also an attraction in itself, offering breathtaking views of the city as it ascends to the park.

Opening Times
The park is open 24 hours a day, seven days a week, making it a perfect spot for both daytime and nighttime visits. However, the operating hours of the attractions within the park may vary.

Tips for Visiting
When visiting Mtatsminda Park, make sure to wear comfortable shoes as there will be a lot of walking. Also, don't forget to bring a camera to capture the stunning views of Tbilisi from the top of the park. Lastly, try to visit the park during the weekdays to avoid the crowds.

6.6 The Georgian National Museum

The Georgian National Museum is a significant cultural and educational institution that was established in 2004. It is the result of the unification of several museums and research centers. The museum hosts various exhibitions, both temporary and permanent, that tell the story of Georgia's history and culture.

The museum's main site is the Simon Janashia Museum of Georgia. This museum is the oldest in Georgia and operates as a scientific-educational institution. It houses a vast collection of artifacts that provide insight into the country's rich history and diverse culture.

The Georgian National Museum is located in the heart of Tbilisi, making it easily accessible for tourists. It's a must-visit for anyone interested in learning more about Georgia's past and present. The museum is open to the public, but it's always a good idea to check the official website for the most up-to-date information on opening hours and any special exhibitions.

Interesting Facts and Tips
The Georgian National Museum is not just one building but a network of 20 museums and cultural institutions. This means that a visit to the museum can take you on a journey across different locations, each offering a unique perspective on Georgian history and culture.
When visiting the museum, it's recommended to set aside a few hours to fully explore the exhibitions. The museum's collections are vast and diverse, ranging from archaeological artifacts to contemporary art.
Please note that the museum's opening hours and rules may vary depending on the current COVID-19 situation. It's recommended to check the official website for the most up-to-date information before planning your visit.

6.7   The Tbilisi Sea

The Tbilisi Sea is a large artificial lake located to the north-east of Tbilisi, the capital city of Georgia. Despite its name, it's not a sea but rather a reservoir. It was created in the 1950s for the purpose of supplying the city with water and electricity. It's called a "sea" because of its large size.

Interesting Facts
The Tbilisi Sea is the largest body of water in Tbilisi. It's a popular spot for locals and tourists alike, especially during the hot summer months. The water is clean and safe for swimming. The area around the lake is also a great place for picnics and outdoor activities. There are also several beaches around the lake where you can relax and enjoy the sun.

Visiting Tips
The best time to visit the Tbilisi Sea is during the summer when the weather is warm and the water is perfect for swimming. There are several public and private beaches around the lake, some of which offer amenities like umbrellas, sunbeds, and cafes. It's a great place to spend a day relaxing and enjoying the beautiful surroundings.

Location and How to Get There
The Tbilisi Sea is located to the north-east of Tbilisi. You can get there by car or by public transportation. There are several buses that go to the Tbilisi Sea from different parts of the city. If you're driving, there's plenty of parking available near the lake.

Opening Times
The Tbilisi Sea is open to the public all year round, but the best time to visit is during the summer months when the weather is warm. The beaches around the lake are usually open from early morning until late in the evening.

6.8 The National Botanical Garden of Georgia

The National Botanical Garden of Georgia, also known as the Tbilisi Botanical Garden, is a historical green space located in the heart of Tbilisi, the capital city of Georgia. The garden is nestled in the Tsavkisistskali Gorge, an area known for its scenic beauty.

History
The garden's history dates back to 1625 when it was a royal garden. It was later expanded and officially established as a botanical garden in 1845. The garden has witnessed various historical events and changes, including the Persian invasion and the transformation of Tbilisi into a modern city. It has been a part of the city's evolution, serving as a testament to its rich history.

Flora and Fauna
The garden is home to more than 3,500 plant species, including 350 trees. It's a biodiversity hotspot, featuring local Georgian flora as well as exotic plants from around the world. The garden also houses a herbarium, a greenhouse, and a seed bank, contributing to the conservation of plant diversity.

Visiting the Garden
The garden is open to visitors throughout the year. It's a perfect place for nature lovers, offering a tranquil escape from the bustling

city. Visitors can enjoy a leisurely walk along the well-maintained paths, explore the diverse plant collections, or simply relax in the peaceful surroundings. The garden also features several monuments and a waterfall, adding to its charm.

Location and How to Get There
The National Botanical Garden of Georgia is located in the old town of Tbilisi, near the Narikala Fortress. It's easily accessible by public transportation. You can take a bus to Rike Park and then ride the cable car to Narikala Fortress. From there, it's a short walk to the garden. Alternatively, you can take a taxi directly to the garden.

Opening Times
The garden is open from 9:00 AM to 6:00 PM daily. It's recommended to check the official website or contact the garden directly for the most accurate and up-to-date information.
Visiting the National Botanical Garden of Georgia is a wonderful way to immerse yourself in nature and learn about the diverse plant life. It's a must-visit attraction for anyone traveling to Tbilisi.

6.9 Abanotubani: A Historic Gem in the Heart of Tbilisi

Abanotubani, located in the heart of Tbilisi, Georgia, is a historic district known for its unique sulfur baths. The name 'Abanotubani' translates to 'bath district', a fitting name for a place that has been a center for public bathing since the city's inception.

History

The history of Abanotubani is deeply intertwined with the history of Tbilisi itself. According to legend, King Vakhtang Gorgasali discovered the hot springs while hunting and decided to build a city around them. This city eventually became Tbilisi, the capital of Georgia. The sulfur baths have been a central part of Tbilisi's culture and lifestyle ever since, attracting locals and tourists alike with their therapeutic properties.

Interesting Facts
The baths are built below ground level with only the brick domes visible from the surface, giving the area a distinctive look. Each bathhouse has its own unique design and architecture, some with intricate mosaics and others with smooth marble interiors. The baths are said to have healing properties, particularly for skin and joint problems.

Visiting Abanotubani
When visiting Abanotubani, you can choose between public and private rooms. The private rooms offer more amenities and are perfect for those seeking a more secluded and relaxing experience. The public baths, on the other hand, provide a more social experience. It's a great way to immerse yourself in local culture.

Location and How to Get There
Abanotubani is located in the old part of Tbilisi, near the Mtkvari River. It's within walking distance of many of the city's main attractions, including the Narikala Fortress and the Tbilisi Botanical Garden. If you're using public transportation, the closest metro station is Avlabari on Line 1. From there, it's about a 15-minute walk to the baths.

Opening Times
The sulfur baths are open 24 hours a day, seven days a week, making them a flexible option for any itinerary. However, it's recommended to visit in the early morning or late evening to avoid the crowds. Visiting Abanotubani is a must when in Tbilisi. It offers a unique opportunity to experience a part of the city's history while enjoying a relaxing bath in the therapeutic sulfur waters.

7   Culture and Entertainment in Tbilisi

7.1   Art Galleries

Here are some of the art galleries you should visit in Tbilisi.

LC Queisser
This gallery was founded by German-born curator Lisa Offermann in 2018. It focuses on contemporary works and presents a balanced programme of Georgian and foreign artists. The gallery is also the co-founder of Tbilisi Residencies and the bilingual publishing initiative Kona Books.

Gallery Artbeat
One of the pioneering contemporary art galleries based in Tbilisi, Georgia, representing mid-career and emerging Georgian artists. The gallery found its permanent home in the heart of Tbilisi in 2017.

E.A. Shared Space
Founded by a curator and writer Elene Abashidze, E.A. Shared Space is a project space situated in front of the national Chancellery building, focusing on contemporary art practices with a strong political dimension. The project space has a curated bookstore and a communal library.

The Why Not Gallery
Founded in 2018 by two friends, artist Gvantsa Jishkariani and curator Ellen Kapanadze with an intention to support young Georgian artists. The gallery welcomes and encourages all sorts of experimentation and trials.

Patara
Patara gallery is an artist-run space, initially located in a busy underground passage in central Tbilisi that changed many sites in a nomadic manner. This small vitrine space utilised as a gallery discovers unknown artists.

Gallery 4710
A contemporary art gallery that opened in 2019. The gallery mainly collaborates with emerging Georgian artists. It aims to function as a discovery platform that introduces local newcomers to a larger, international public.

Maudi
Maudi is a multifunctional space for contemporary art, founded by a team of architects – Lado Shonia and Dimitri Eristavi – and curator Liza Zhvania. The exhibition space is situated in the Soviet industrial heritage building named after the material 'maudi' (broadcloth) manufactured there.

Please note that the opening times and entrance fees may vary, so it's recommended to check the galleries' official websites or contact them directly for the most accurate information. Enjoy your visit to these wonderful art galleries in Tbilisi!

7.2 Museums

Here are some of the best museums you can visit in Tbilisi.

Georgian National Museum
Located on Rustaveli Avenue, this museum is a must-visit for anyone interested in Georgian history and culture. It houses a vast collection of artifacts, from ancient gold jewelry to medieval Christian art. The museum's highlight is the Archaeological Treasury, which displays gold and silver artifacts from the pre-Christian period. The museum is open from 10:00 to 18:00, Tuesday through Sunday. The entrance fee is 15 GEL. Visit their official website at www.museum.ge for more details on exhibits and events.

Museum of Georgia
Also located on Rustaveli Avenue, the Museum of Georgia is another great place to learn about the country's history. The museum's collection includes archaeological, ethnographic, and medieval artifacts. The museum is open from 10:00 to 18:00, Tuesday through Sunday. The entrance fee is 7 GEL. For further information, head over to their official website, www.museum.ge.

Tbilisi History Museum: Situated in the old part of the city, this museum offers a glimpse into Tbilisi's past. The museum's collection includes photographs, maps, and other items that tell the story of the city's development. The museum is open from 10:00 to 18:00, Tuesday through Sunday. The entrance fee is 5 GEL. www.tbilisihistorymuseum.ge

Art Museum of Georgia

This museum, located on Rustaveli Avenue, houses one of the largest collections of Georgian art. It features works from the Middle Ages to the present day, including paintings, sculptures, and graphic art. The museum is open from 10:00 to 18:00, Tuesday through Sunday. The entrance fee is 10 GEL. Their official website www.artmuseum.ge offers more information about the collections.

Museum of Soviet Occupation
This museum offers a sobering look at Georgia's history under Soviet rule. The exhibits include personal testimonies, photographs, and documents from the period. The museum is located on Rustaveli Avenue and is open from 10:00 to 18:00, Tuesday through Sunday. The entrance fee is 7 GEL.

7.3 Theatres

Here are some of the best theatres you can visit in Tbilisi.

Rezo Gabriadze Marionette Theater
This unique theatre is home to the works of Rezo Gabriadze, a renowned Georgian artist, writer, and director. The theatre is famous for its marionette performances, which are a blend of drama, tragicomedy, and animation. The theatre is located in the old town of Tbilisi, near the Anchiskhati Basilica. Ticket prices vary depending on the performance, so it's best to check their official website for the most accurate information.

Movement Theatre
This avant-garde theatre is known for its innovative performances that combine music, mime, dance, and circus elements. The theatre is located in the Vera district of Tbilisi. Ticket prices range from 10 to 20 GEL.

Tbilisi Opera and Ballet State Theatre
This historic theatre is one of the oldest in Eastern Europe and is a must-visit for fans of opera and ballet. The theatre is located on Rustaveli Avenue, one of the main thoroughfares in Tbilisi. Ticket prices vary depending on the performance.

Rhike Park – Music Theatre and Exhibition Hall

This modern architectural marvel is home to a music theatre and an exhibition hall. The complex is located in Rhike Park, along the Mtkvari River. The music theatre hosts a variety of performances, including concerts and musicals. Ticket prices vary depending on the event.

Rustaveli Theatre
Named after the medieval Georgian poet, Shota Rustaveli, this theatre is one of the most important cultural sites in Georgia. The theatre hosts a variety of performances, including plays, musicals, and ballets. It's located on Rustaveli Avenue. Ticket prices vary depending on the performance.

Please note that the opening times and ticket prices are subject to change, so it's always a good idea to check the theatres' official websites before your visit.

7.4 Nightlife in Tbilisi

Here are some of the best places to experience the nightlife in Tbilisi.

Shardeni Street
Located in the center of the old city, Shardeni Street is a hotspot for Tbilisi's nightlife. Here you will find many restaurants and bars where you can enjoy a variety of cuisines and drinks. It's a great place to start your night out in Tbilisi.

Bassiani
Bassiani is one of the top nightlife spots in Tbilisi. It's known for its vibrant music scene and is a popular destination for dance music lovers.

KHIDI
KHIDI is another great place for nightlife in Tbilisi. It offers a unique experience with its underground music and industrial setting.

Fabrika
Fabrika is a multi-functional urban space in Tbilisi where locals and tourists gather for a variety of cultural events. It's a great place to meet new people and experience the local culture.

Dance Clubs & Discos

Tbilisi has a number of dance clubs and discos where you can dance the night away. Some popular ones include Hubble, Cafe Gallery Club, Blow Bar, SAFE Club, Bassiani, The Bank Club, Candy, and Parampa.

Wine Bars

Tbilisi is also known for its wine bars. Some recommended ones include Odo's Space, Patara Dzagli, Wine Spot Ghvinisi, Gamarjoba Wine Store, and 41 Gradus. These places offer a wide selection of Georgian wines that you can try.

Lucy Tattoo Studio

While not a traditional nightlife spot, Lucy Tattoo Studio is a unique place to visit in Tbilisi. It's a tattoo studio by day and a bar by night, offering a unique blend of art and nightlife.

Remember, the nightlife in Tbilisi can be vibrant and exciting, but it's important to stay safe and respect the local customs and laws. Enjoy your time exploring the city after dark!

Please note that opening times and entrance fees may vary, so it's always a good idea to check the official websites or contact the venues directly for the most accurate and up-to-date information.

8 Day Trips and Excursions

8.1 One Day in Tbilisi Itinerary

Below is a suggestion for a detailed itinerary for spending one day in Tbilisi, starting at 08:00 and ending at 23:00.

08:00 - 10:00: Visit the Old Town
Start your day by exploring the Old Town, the most historical part of Tbilisi. Wander around the streets and admire the beautiful colorful buildings and balconies. Don't miss the Clock Tower and the Chreli Abano (Thermal Bath). If you have time, you can also visit the sulfur bath, one of the most popular activities in the city.

10:00 - 12:00: Discover the New City
After exploring the Old Town, head to the Bridge of Peace towards the New City. The Bridge of Peace unites the Old Town with the New City and offers great views over the river Mtkvari (Kura). Here you can also buy some local souvenirs and have a cup of coffee in a nice coffee shop.

12:00 - 14:00: Take the cable car to the top
Next, head to the cable car to see the city from above. To get to the top, you will need to purchase a card which costs 2 Lari. This is also the ideal place to have lunch. The restaurant 'Funicular' not only overlooks the whole city, but also serves some of the best Adjarian Khachapuri in the whole city. This is a so-called 'cheeseboat' – bread filled with cheese, some butter and an egg. It is eaten by tearing off the bread and dipping it in the cheese sauce. It is a must-try dish in Georgia!

14:00 - 16:00: Visit the Holy Trinity Cathedral
You cannot leave Tbilisi without visiting any of the cathedrals – this is why the Holy Trinity Cathedral is a must. You can take a taxi from the cable car point (taxis are very cheap in Georgia), and you will be there in less than 20 minutes. Before going to the cathedral, make sure that you wear a skirt/dress if you are a female and bring a headscarf to wear. These are usually provided, but it is usually best to bring your own. Nothing is required for men.

16:00 - 18:00: Have drinks at Fabrika

Fabrika is a popular hostel where young people gather every evening to hang out and have drinks. The vibe here is very alive every day – even during the week! It is definitely worth coming here if you fancy meeting some locals and maybe having a few drinks.

18:00 - 20:00: Khinkali dinner

There are many amazing and fancy restaurants in Tbilisi. However, 'Khinkali house' is one of my favorites because it is open 24/7 and serves very affordable and delicious food. Khinkali (the Georgian dumplings) are a must as well, so what better way to finish off a full day of activities than with a feast?

20:00 - 23:00: Explore Tbilisi at night

Spend the rest of your evening exploring Tbilisi at night. The city is beautifully lit up and offers a different atmosphere compared to the daytime. You can take a leisurely stroll around the city or visit one of the many bars or clubs if you're in the mood for some nightlife.

For more details, you can visit the source. Please note that the times are approximate and can vary depending on your pace and interest. Enjoy your trip to Tbilisi!

8.1.1   Map for 1 Day in Tbilisi

Interactive link to the map: https://bit.ly/tbilisioneday

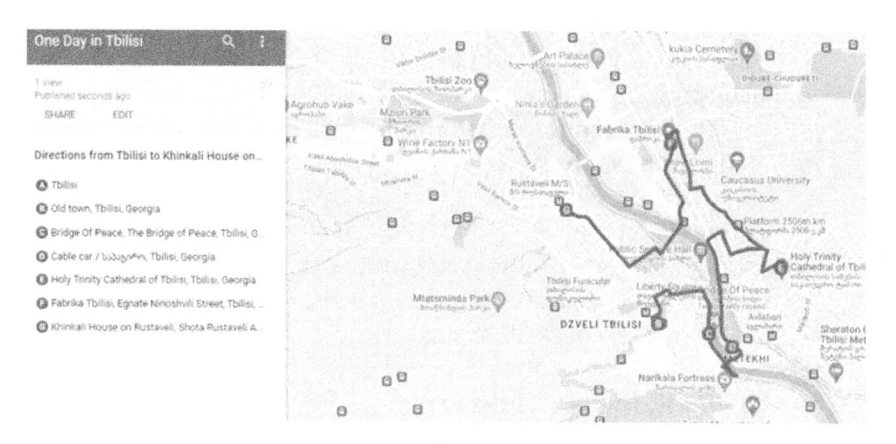

8.2   Tbilisi: Kazbegi Full-Day Group Tour

This full-day group tour is a fantastic way to explore the stunning landscapes of Kazbegi and the Gergeti Trinity Church, which are surrounded by magical mountain peaks and breathtaking valleys. You'll also get to experience the spectacular slopes of Gudauri and delve into the history of the Ananuri Fortress.

08:00 - Departure from Tbilisi
Start your day early and meet your tour group in Tbilisi. From there, you'll embark on your journey towards Kazbegi.

10:00 - Ananuri Fortress
Your first stop will be at the historical Ananuri Fortress. This fortress is a place of historical significance and offers a glimpse into Georgia's past. Spend some time exploring the fortress and learning about its history.

12:00 - Gudauri
Next, you'll head to the slopes of Gudauri. This ski resort is known for its stunning views and outdoor activities. Even if you're not skiing, you can still enjoy the beautiful scenery and take some amazing photos.

14:00 - Lunch
Take a break and enjoy a local meal. This is a great opportunity to try some traditional Georgian cuisine.

15:00 - Gergeti Trinity Church
After lunch, you'll head to the Gergeti Trinity Church. This church is located at an elevation of 2170 meters, under Mount Kazbegi. The church is a popular waypoint for trekkers in the area, and is widely recognized symbol of Georgia.

17:00 - Kazbegi
Spend the rest of the afternoon exploring Kazbegi. This area is known for its stunning landscapes, so be sure to take some time to appreciate the natural beauty.

19:00 - Return to Tbilisi
As the day comes to an end, you'll head back to Tbilisi. This is a great time to reflect on the day's adventures and share your favorite moments with your fellow travelers.

23:00 - Arrival in Tbilisi

You'll arrive back in Tbilisi late in the evening, marking the end of your full-day tour.

This tour is a bestseller and has received a rating of 4.9 out of 5 from 938 reviews. The starting price is $33.15 per person, which is a 15% discount from the base price of $39.00. The tour includes free cancellation.

For more information and to book your spot, visit the official tour page at https://bit.ly/3Dihfpc.

Please note that the itinerary may vary depending on the tour operator and weather conditions. Always check the details provided by the tour operator before your trip.

8.2.1 Map for Tbilisi: Kazbegi Full-Day Group Tour

Interactive link of the map.: https://bit.ly/3JZqsa0

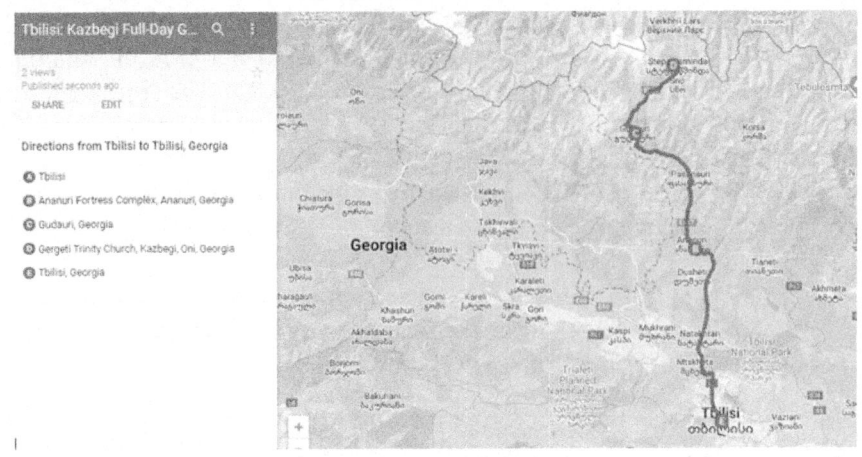

8.3 From Tbilisi: Day Trip to Armenia Including Homemade Lunch

Here is the detailed itinerary for the tour titled "From Tbilisi: Day Trip to Armenia Including Homemade Lunch".

08:00 - Departure from Tbilisi
Start your day early with a departure from Tbilisi. Make sure to bring along your passport as you'll be crossing the border into Armenia.

10:00 - Arrival in Armenia
Upon arrival in Armenia, you'll be greeted by the stunning landscapes of this beautiful country.

11:00 - Sightseeing
Spend the next few hours sightseeing. You'll have the opportunity to explore the local attractions, including the spectacular slopes of Gudauri and the historical Ananuri Fortress.

13:00 - Homemade Lunch
Enjoy a delicious homemade lunch, giving you a taste of authentic Armenian cuisine. This is a great opportunity to experience the local culture and hospitality.

14:00 - More Sightseeing

After lunch, continue your sightseeing tour. There's plenty to see in this beautiful country, so make the most of your time here.

18:00 - Departure to Tbilisi
As the day comes to an end, you'll depart Armenia and head back to Tbilisi.

20:00 - Arrival in Tbilisi
You'll arrive back in Tbilisi in the evening, giving you plenty of time to rest and reflect on your day of adventure.

23:00 - End of the Day
Your day ends here. Rest well for your next day of exploration.

Please note that this is a general itinerary and the actual schedule might vary based on the tour operator's plan and the traffic conditions of the day. The tour includes a full day of activities, so make sure to wear comfortable shoes and clothing.

The tour starts at $33.15 per person and you can book it here.

8.3.1   Map of Day Trip to Armenia Including Homemade Lunch

Interactive link to the map: https://bit.ly/43sqFJr

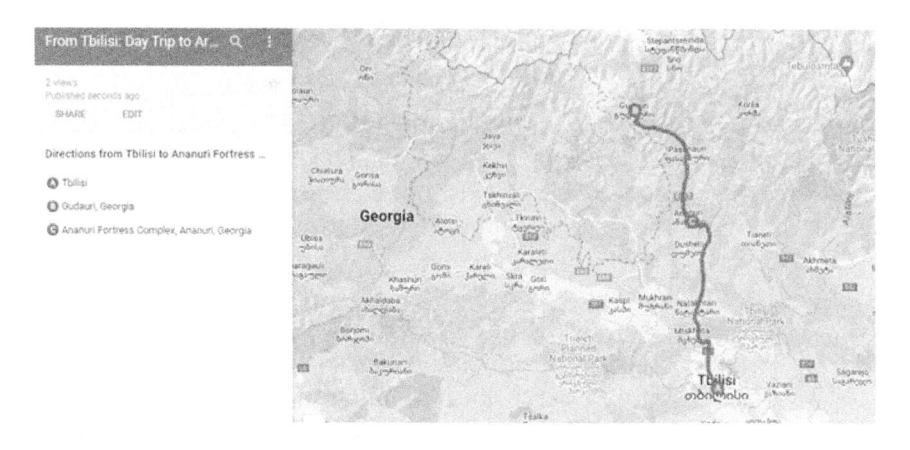

8.4   Tbilisi: Jvari Monastery, Ananuri, Gudauri, and Kazbegi Tour

Sure, here's a detailed itinerary for the "Tbilisi: Jvari Monastery, Ananuri, Gudauri, and Kazbegi Tour". This tour is a full-day adventure that takes you to some of the most beautiful and historic sites in Georgia.

08:00 - Departure from Tbilisi
Your day begins with an 8:00 AM departure from Tbilisi. Make sure to have a hearty breakfast before you leave, as it's going to be a long day full of exciting activities.

09:30 - Jvari Monastery
Your first stop is the **Jvari Monastery**, a 6th-century Georgian Orthodox monastery near Mtskheta, eastern Georgia. Standing on the rocky mountaintop at the confluence of the Mtkvari and Aragvi rivers, the monastery provides stunning views of the surrounding landscape.

11:00 - Ananuri Fortress
Next, you'll head to the **Ananuri Fortress**, a castle complex on the Aragvi River. Explore the fortress and learn about its rich history. Don't forget to take some photos of the stunning views of the river and surrounding mountains.

13:00 - Lunch
You'll have a break for lunch. You can bring your own or try some local Georgian cuisine at a nearby restaurant.

14:30 - Gudauri
After lunch, you'll continue to **Gudauri**, a popular ski resort located on the south-facing plateau of The Greater Caucasus Mountain Range. Even if you're not skiing, you can enjoy the breathtaking views of the Caucasus Mountains.

16:00 - Kazbegi
The final stop of the day is **Kazbegi**, a small town in the Mtskheta-Mtianeti region of north-eastern Georgia. Here, you'll visit the Gergeti Trinity Church, located under Mount Kazbegi. The church is a popular waypoint for trekkers in the area, and can be reached by a steep 3 hour climb up the mountain, or around 30 minutes by jeep up a rough mountain trail.

19:00 - Return to Tbilisi

After a full day of exploring, you'll return to Tbilisi. You can use this time to relax and reflect on the day's adventures.

21:00 - Dinner in Tbilisi
Once you're back in Tbilisi, consider having dinner at one of the city's many excellent restaurants. Georgian cuisine is renowned for its unique flavors and techniques, so this is a perfect opportunity to try dishes like khachapuri (cheese-filled bread) or khinkali (Georgian dumplings).

23:00 - End of the Day
After dinner, you can choose to explore Tbilisi's nightlife or head back to your accommodation to rest.

Please note that this is a rough itinerary and the actual schedule might vary depending on the tour operator. The tour price starts from **US$ 49 per person**. You can book the tour and find more details here.
Remember to wear comfortable shoes as there will be a fair amount of walking involved. Also, don't forget to bring a camera to capture the stunning views you'll encounter throughout the day!

8.4.1 Tbilisi: Jvari Monastery, Ananuri, Gudauri, and Kazbegi Tour

Interactive link to the map: https://bit.ly/3rz1nfx

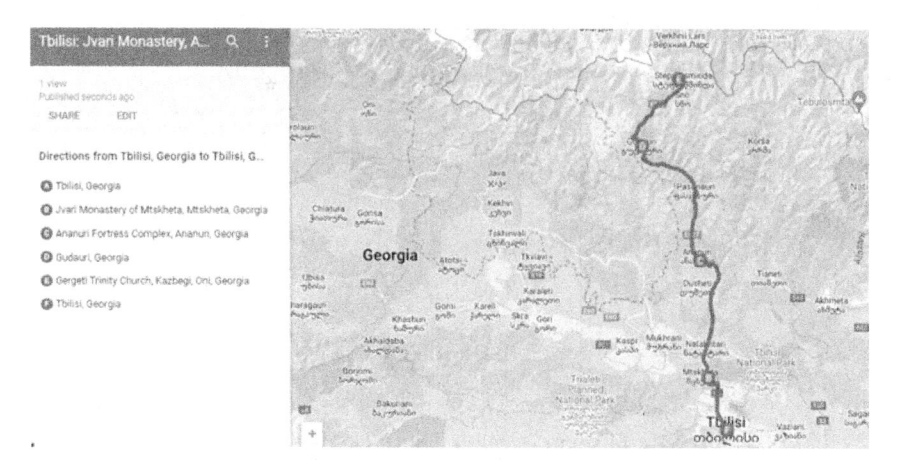

9 3 Days in Tbilisi

Here's a detailed itinerary for a three-day tour in Tbilisi.

9.1 Day One

08:00 - Breakfast at your hotel
Start your day with a hearty breakfast at your hotel. Tbilisi offers a variety of local and international cuisines. Try some traditional Georgian dishes like Khachapuri (cheese-filled bread) or Khinkali (dumplings).

09:00 - Visit the Holy Trinity Cathedral
Begin your sightseeing with a visit to the Holy Trinity Cathedral, also known as Sameba. It's one of the largest Orthodox cathedrals in the world and offers stunning views of the city.

10:30 - Explore the Old Town
Next, head to the Old Town, a maze of narrow streets where wooden balconies look down from old brick-build homes. Don't miss the Clock Tower, a quirky leaning tower that houses a small theatre.

12:00 - Lunch at a local restaurant
Have lunch at one of the local restaurants in the Old Town. Try some more Georgian dishes like Lobio (bean soup) or Mtsvadi (Georgian shashlik).

13:30 - Visit the Georgian National Museum
After lunch, visit the Georgian National Museum. The museum houses a vast collection of art and cultural artifacts that tell the story of Georgia's history.

15:00 - Stroll down Rustaveli Avenue
Take a leisurely stroll down Rustaveli Avenue, the main street in Tbilisi.
You'll find a mix of modern and Soviet-era architecture, as well as a number of shops and cafes.

16:30 - Visit the National Opera and Ballet Theatre
Stop by the National Opera and Ballet Theatre, a beautiful building with an impressive interior. If you're a fan of performing arts, consider catching a show in the evening.

18:00 - Dinner at a local restaurant
Have dinner at one of the local restaurants on Rustaveli Avenue. Georgian cuisine is a highlight of any visit to the country, so make sure to try as many dishes as you can.

20:00 - Take a walk in Rike Park and cross the Peace Bridge
After dinner, take a walk in Rike Park and cross the Peace Bridge, a modern glass and steel construction that offers great views of the city.

21:30 - Take the cable car to Narikala Fortress
The fortress itself is mostly in ruins, but it offers the best panoramic view of Tbilisi, especially stunning at night.

23:00 - Return to your hotel
After a long day of sightseeing, return to your hotel for a good night's sleep. You'll need to rest up for another exciting day in Tbilisi!

Please note that the times are approximate and can vary depending on your pace and interest. Also, it's always a good idea to check the opening hours of the attractions as they can change. Enjoy your trip to Tbilisi!

9.1.1 Map of Day One in Tbilisi

Interactive link to the map: https://bit.ly/44N71ck

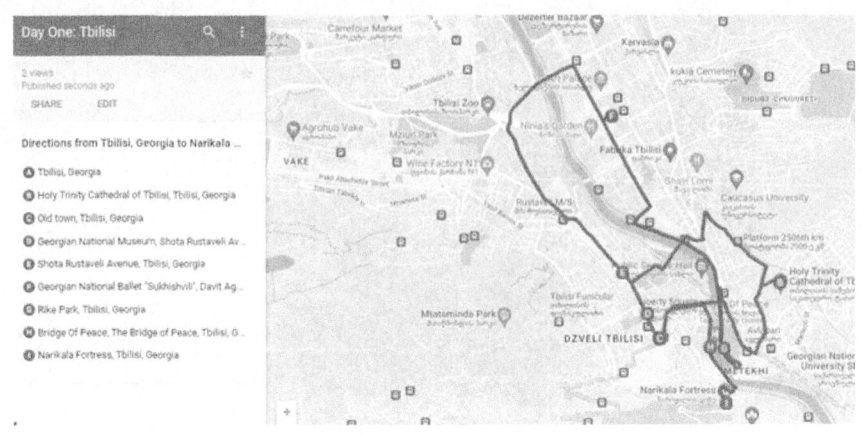

9.2 Day Two

08:00 - Breakfast at your hotel
Start your day with a hearty breakfast at your hotel.

09:00 - Visit the Dry Bridge Market
The Dry Bridge Market, a sprawling flea market where you can find a wide range of items from Soviet memorabilia to jewelry and artwork.

11:30 - Visit the Tbilisi History Museum
The Tbilisi History Museum which has a great collection of art and historical artifacts.

13:00 - Lunch at a local restaurant
Have lunch at one of the local restaurants in the Marjanishvili area.

14:30 – Marjanishvili Area
After lunch, explore the Marjanishvili area. This part of Tbilisi is a lot less touristy and is a great place to explore local shops and restaurants.

16:30 – Fabrika
Finish your day at Fabrika, a former Soviet sewing factory that has been transformed into a multi-purpose space with bars, restaurants, shops, and a hostel.

9.2.1 Map of Day Two in Tbilisi

Interactive link to the map: https://bit.ly/3rH0Qbi

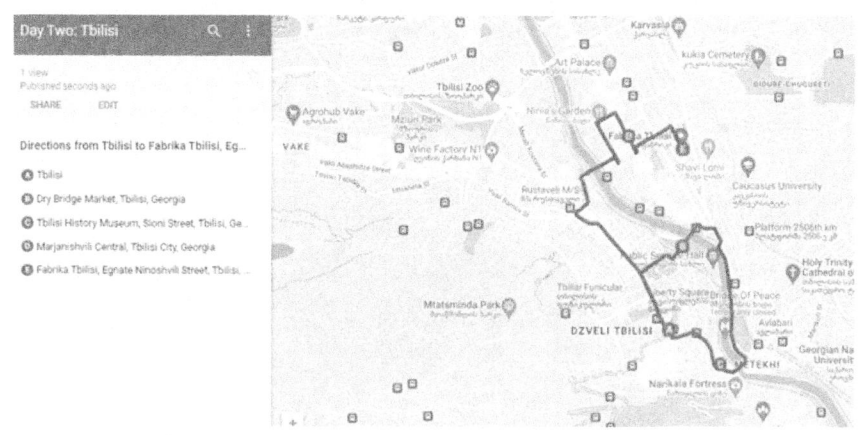

9.3 Day Three

08:00 - Breakfast at your hotel
Start your day with a hearty breakfast at your hotel.

09:00 - Visit the Tbilisi Sea
Begin your day at the Tbilisi Sea, a large artificial lake located to the east of the city. It's a popular spot for locals during the summer months.

12:00 – Head to the Chronicles of Georgia
After spending some time at the lake, head to the Chronicles of Georgia. These massive stone pillars tell the story of Georgia's history and are located in a beautiful setting overlooking the Tbilisi Sea.

13:00 – Head over to Mtatsminda Park
Have lunch at the park.

14:30 – Mtatsminda Park
After lunch, enjoy the funfair located at the top of Mount Mtatsminda. You can reach the park by taking the funicular from the city center.

9.3.1 Map of Day Three in Tbilisi

Interactive link to the map: https://bit.ly/3Q2kZ5O

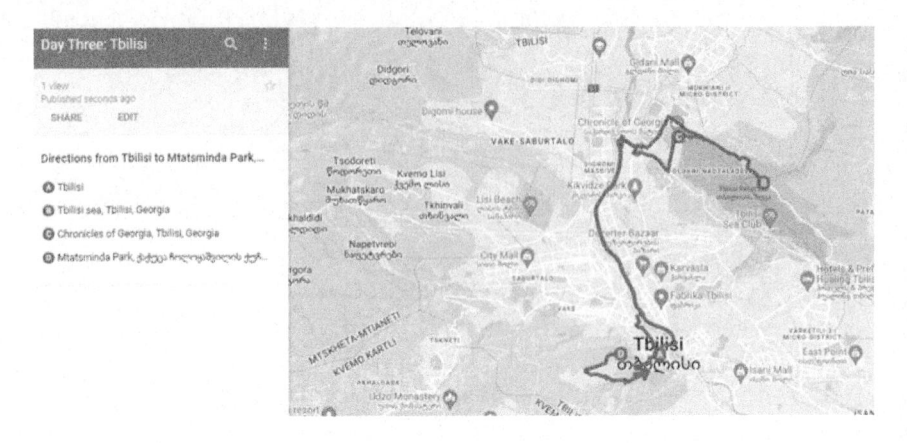

10 Practical Tips for Visiting Tbilisi

In summary, here are some practical tips for first-time travelers to Tbilisi.

10.1 Currency

The currency in Georgia is the Georgian Lari (GEL). It's always a good idea to have some local currency on hand for small purchases, although credit cards are widely accepted in most places.

10.2 Language

The official language is Georgian. While English is not widely spoken by the older population, younger Georgians and those working in tourism generally speak good English. It might be helpful to learn a few basic Georgian phrases.

10.3 Safety

Tbilisi is generally a safe city for tourists. However, like in any other city, it's important to be aware of your surroundings, especially at night, and keep an eye on your belongings.

10.4 Dress Code

Georgians are quite fashionable. In Tbilisi, you can dress as you would in any other European city. However, if you plan to visit any churches or monasteries, women are often required to cover their heads with a scarf and both men and women need to cover their knees.

10.5 Transportation

Tbilisi has a good public transportation system, including buses, minibuses, a metro system, and cable cars. Taxis are also quite affordable. You can use apps like Bolt or Yandex for a taxi.

10.6 Food and Water

Georgian cuisine is delicious and diverse. Be sure to try dishes like khachapuri (cheese-filled bread) and khinkali (dumplings). Tap water in Tbilisi is safe to drink, but if you prefer, bottled water is widely available.

10.7 Connectivity

Free Wi-Fi is available in many public areas, cafes, and restaurants in Tbilisi. If you need a reliable internet connection, consider getting a local SIM card.

10.8 Weather

Tbilisi has a humid subtropical climate with considerable continental influences. The city experiences hot summers and moderately cold winters. Depending on the time of your visit, pack accordingly.

10.9 Sightseeing

Tbilisi is rich in history and culture. Don't miss the old town, the Narikala Fortress, the Holy Trinity Cathedral, and the Dry Bridge Flea Market. Also, consider taking day trips to nearby areas like Mtskheta, Kazbegi, and the Kakheti wine region.

10.10 Respect Local Customs

Georgians are known for their hospitality. Respect local traditions and customs, and you'll be warmly welcomed.

11   Conclusion

As we wrap up this comprehensive guide to Tbilisi, it's clear that this vibrant city is a treasure trove of cultural experiences, historical landmarks, and culinary delights. From its cobblestone streets and ancient architecture to its modern cafes and bustling markets, Tbilisi offers a unique blend of old and new that captivates every visitor.

Tbilisi is a city where every corner tells a story. Its rich history is reflected in its diverse architecture, from the ancient Narikala Fortress and the stunning Sameba Cathedral to the charming old town and the futuristic Bridge of Peace. The city's museums and art galleries offer a deeper understanding of Georgia's complex history and vibrant culture.

The city's culinary scene is another highlight of any visit to Tbilisi. With its unique blend of flavors from Europe, Asia, and the Middle East, Georgian cuisine is a gastronomic adventure. Whether you're tasting khinkali at a local tavern or savoring a glass of traditional Georgian wine, your taste buds are in for a treat.

Tbilisi's natural beauty is also a major draw for visitors. The city's parks and gardens offer tranquil retreats from the hustle and bustle, while the nearby mountains and canyons offer thrilling adventures for outdoor enthusiasts. And let's not forget the city's famous sulfur baths, a perfect way to relax and unwind after a day of exploration.

But what truly sets Tbilisi apart is its people. Georgians are known for their warm hospitality, and visitors to Tbilisi often remark on the friendliness and generosity of the locals. It's this spirit of hospitality that makes a visit to Tbilisi more than just a trip—it's an experience that touches the heart.

Whether you're a history buff, a foodie, an art lover, or an adventurer, Tbilisi has something for everyone. With its rich history, vibrant culture, delicious food, and stunning landscapes, Tbilisi is a destination that deserves a spot on every traveler's bucket list.

As we conclude this guide, we hope that it has provided you with a useful roadmap for your journey to Tbilisi. But remember, the best way to discover Tbilisi is to explore it for yourself. So pack your bags, open your mind, and get ready for an unforgettable adventure in Tbilisi. Safe travels!